# Make Time
*Daily Devotional Journal*

© LDS Living

This material is neither made, provided, approved, nor endorsed by Intellectual Reserve, Inc. or The Church of Jesus Christ of Latter-day Saints. Any content or opinions expressed, implied or included in or with the material are solely those of the owner and not those of Intellectual Reserve, Inc. or The Church of Jesus Christ of Latter-day Saints.

ISBN: 978-1-63993-251-1
Printed in China

# Make Time
## *Daily Devotional Journal*

 magnify

# *An Invitation*

"I plead with you to make time for the Lord! Make your own spiritual foundation firm and able to stand the test of time by doing those things that allow the Holy Ghost to be with you *always*. . . .

"The Lord knows you and loves you. He is your Savior and your Redeemer. He leads and guides His Church. He will lead and guide *you* in your personal life if you will *make time for Him* in your life—each and every day" (Russell M. Nelson, "Make Time for the Lord," October 2021).

With our full plates and busy schedules, we can forget to prioritize the very thing that will empower us to navigate and handle those plates and schedules—time with Christ.

Though this journal is not a replacement for scripture study, it is an accessible and effective way to make turning to Christ a daily habit. By taking a quick minute each day to read a scripture and a quote, followed by a pause for reflection, we can consistently build our relationship with Christ and His gospel, one simple sermon and one day at a time. Let's do it!

## HOW IT WORKS

On each page of this journal there is a scripture with a corresponding quote from general conference—what we call the daily devotional for each day. The page ends with a few questions to help you reflect, connect, and create a daily practice. The whole process can take less than five minutes.

At the recommended rate of one page per day, this journal will last an entire year. Never stress if you miss a day (or a few)—just jump back in where you left off. This journaling practice is about intentionally making time for Christ, not creating a perfect participation streak.

## WHY IT WORKS

We have been promised time and time again, through both ancient and modern scripture, that our efforts matter, no matter how small.

"By small and simple things are great things brought to pass"—Alma 37:6.

"The Lord loves effort. The Lord loves consistency. The Lord loves steadfastness. While we surely will come up short from time to time, our persistent efforts to hear Him and follow the inspiration He gives us will help us to 'wax strong in the Spirit'" (Russell M. Nelson, Facebook message, 1 January 2022).

Choosing to spend time with the Lord and using our energy to intentionally come closer to Him—even when the effort is small—has a large impact. Even a few minutes spent focusing on Christ shifts our mindset, strengthens our faith, and empowers us to partner with Him in all we face.

We could all use a little more Jesus—let's get there one day at a time!

DATE      /      /

## Scripture of the Day

"Charity suffereth long, and is kind; charity envieth not; charity vaunteth not itself, is not puffed up, doth not behave itself unseemly, seeketh not her own, is not easily provoked, thinketh no evil."

*1 Corinthians 13:4–5*

## Quote of the Day

*Ulisses Soares, "Followers of the Prince of Peace," April 2023*

"As we strive to develop attributes like the Savior's, we can become instruments of His peace in the world according to the pattern that He Himself established. I invite you to consider ways we can transform ourselves into uplifting and supportive people, people who have an understanding and forgiving heart, people who look for the best in others, always remembering that 'if there is anything virtuous, lovely, or of good report or praiseworthy, we seek after these things.'"

### HOW DID GOD SHOW UP FOR YOU TODAY?

### WHAT CAN YOU ASK CHRIST TO HELP YOU CARRY RIGHT NOW?

### WHAT IS YOUR HOPE FOR TOMORROW?

DATE      /      /

**Scripture of the Day**

*Matthew 11:28*

"Come unto me, all ye that labour and are heavy laden, and I will give you rest."

**Quote of the Day**

*Alvin F. Meredith III, "Look down the Road," October 2021*

"We may pray that if the help will not come immediately, it will at least come in the second watch or even the third watch of the proverbial night. When we must wait, rest assured that the Savior is always watching, ensuring that we will not have to endure more than we can bear."

### HOW DID GOD SHOW UP FOR YOU TODAY?

### WHAT CAN YOU ASK CHRIST TO HELP YOU CARRY RIGHT NOW?

### WHAT IS YOUR HOPE FOR TOMORROW?

DATE    /    /

## *Scripture of the Day*

"As ye have therefore received Christ Jesus the Lord, so walk ye in him."

*Colossians 2:6*

## *Quote of the Day*

"To *do justly* means acting honorably with God and with other people. We act honorably with God by walking humbly with Him. We act honorably with others by loving mercy."

*Dale G. Renlund, "Do Justly, Love Mercy, and Walk Humbly with God," October 2020*

### HOW DID GOD SHOW UP FOR YOU TODAY?

### WHAT CAN YOU ASK CHRIST TO HELP YOU CARRY RIGHT NOW?

### WHAT IS YOUR HOPE FOR TOMORROW?

DATE     /     /

## Scripture of the Day

*Alma 37:6*

"I say unto you, that by small and simple things are great things brought to pass."

## Quote of the Day

*Gary E. Stevenson, "Simply Beautiful—Beautifully Simple," October 2021*

"Jesus Christ Himself describes that His yoke is easy and His burden is light. We should all strive to keep the gospel simple—in our lives, in our families, in our classes and quorums, and in our wards and stakes."

### HOW DID GOD SHOW UP FOR YOU TODAY?

### WHAT CAN YOU ASK CHRIST TO HELP YOU CARRY RIGHT NOW?

### WHAT IS YOUR HOPE FOR TOMORROW?

DATE        /        /

## Scripture of the Day

*Mosiah 4:9*

"Believe in God; believe that he is, and that he created all things, both in heaven and in earth; believe that he has all wisdom, and all power, both in heaven and in earth; believe that man doth not comprehend all the things which the Lord can comprehend."

## Quote of the Day

*W. Mark Bassett, "After the Fourth Day," April 2023*

"When the Savior arrived in Bethany, all had lost hope that Lazarus could be saved—it had been four days, and he was gone. Sometimes during our own challenges, we might feel like Christ is too late, and our hope and faith might even feel challenged. My witness and testimony are that as we move forward with faith in Jesus Christ, the fourth day will always come. He will always come to our aid or to raise our hopes back to life."

### HOW DID GOD SHOW UP FOR YOU TODAY?

### WHAT CAN YOU ASK CHRIST TO HELP YOU CARRY RIGHT NOW?

### WHAT IS YOUR HOPE FOR TOMORROW?

DATE    /    /

## Scripture of the Day

*Doctrine and Covenants 11:25*

"Deny not the spirit of revelation, nor the spirit of prophecy, for wo unto him that denieth these things."

## Quote of the Day

*Allen D. Haynie, "A Living Prophet for the Latter Days," April 2023*

"Knowing by revelation that there is a living prophet on the earth changes everything. . . . After all, a perfect and loving Father in Heaven has chosen the pattern of revealing truth to His children through a prophet, someone who never sought such a sacred calling and who has no need of our help to be aware of his own imperfections. A prophet is someone God has personally prepared, called, corrected, inspired, rebuked, sanctified, and sustained. That is why we are never spiritually at risk in following prophetic counsel."

### HOW DID GOD SHOW UP FOR YOU TODAY?

### WHAT CAN YOU ASK CHRIST TO HELP YOU CARRY RIGHT NOW?

### WHAT IS YOUR HOPE FOR TOMORROW?

DATE  /  /

## Scripture of the Day

*Psalm 136:26*

"O give thanks unto the God of heaven: for his mercy endureth for ever."

## Quote of the Day

*Ulisses Soares, "The Savior's Abiding Compassion," October 2021*

"Many people within our circle of influence are seeking comfort, attention, inclusion, and any help that we can offer them. We all can be instruments in the Lord's hands and act compassionately toward those in need, just as Jesus did."

### HOW DID GOD SHOW UP FOR YOU TODAY?

### WHAT CAN YOU ASK CHRIST TO HELP YOU CARRY RIGHT NOW?

### WHAT IS YOUR HOPE FOR TOMORROW?

DATE      /      /

## *Scripture of the Day*

*Luke 8:48*

"Daughter, be of good comfort: thy faith hath made thee whole; go in peace."

## *Quote of the Day*

*Amy A. Wright, "Christ Heals That Which Is Broken," April 2022*

"Often the scriptures give only a small portion of someone's life, and based on that portion, we sometimes tend to exalt or condemn. No one's life can be understood by one magnificent moment or one regrettable public disappointment. The purpose of these scriptural accounts is to help us see that Jesus Christ was the answer then, and He is the answer now. He knows our complete story and exactly what we suffer, as well as our capabilities and vulnerabilities."

### HOW DID GOD SHOW UP FOR YOU TODAY?

### WHAT CAN YOU ASK CHRIST TO HELP YOU CARRY RIGHT NOW?

### WHAT IS YOUR HOPE FOR TOMORROW?

DATE    /    /

## Scripture of the Day

"My grace is sufficient for thee: for my strength is made perfect in weakness."

*2 Corinthians 12:9*

## Quote of the Day

"There may be other times when we recognize a need but feel inadequate to respond, assuming that what we have to offer is insufficient. To do just as He did, however, is to minister by giving what we are capable of giving and to trust that the Lord will magnify our efforts."

*W. Christopher Waddell, "Just as He Did," April 2019*

### HOW DID GOD SHOW UP FOR YOU TODAY?

### WHAT CAN YOU ASK CHRIST TO HELP YOU CARRY RIGHT NOW?

### WHAT IS YOUR HOPE FOR TOMORROW?

DATE    /    /

## Scripture of the Day

"Neither do I condemn thee: go, and sin no more."

*John 8:11*

## Quote of the Day

"Forgiveness sets us free and makes us worthy to partake of the sacrament every Sunday. Forgiveness is required for us to be truly disciples of Jesus Christ."

*Alfred Kyungu, "To Be a Follower of Christ," October 2021*

### HOW DID GOD SHOW UP FOR YOU TODAY?

### WHAT CAN YOU ASK CHRIST TO HELP YOU CARRY RIGHT NOW?

### WHAT IS YOUR HOPE FOR TOMORROW?

DATE       /       /

## Scripture of the Day

*3 Nephi 12:48*

"Therefore I would that ye should be perfect even as I, or your Father who is in heaven is perfect."

## Quote of the Day

*Vern P. Stanfill, "The Imperfect Harvest," April 2023*

"We must remember that whatever our best-but-imperfect offering is, the Savior can make it perfect. No matter how insignificant our efforts may seem, we must never underestimate the Savior's power."

### HOW DID GOD SHOW UP FOR YOU TODAY?

### WHAT CAN YOU ASK CHRIST TO HELP YOU CARRY RIGHT NOW?

### WHAT IS YOUR HOPE FOR TOMORROW?

DATE    /    /

## Scripture of the Day

*Doctrine and Covenants 19:16*

"For behold, I, God, have suffered these things for all, that they might not suffer if they would repent."

## Quote of the Day

*Matthew S. Holland, "The Exquisite Gift of the Son," October 2020*

"We must never forget that the very purpose of repentance is to take certain misery and transform it into pure bliss. Thanks to His 'immediate goodness,' the *instant* we come unto Christ—demonstrating faith in Him and a true change of heart—the crushing weight of our sins starts to shift from our backs to His."

### HOW DID GOD SHOW UP FOR YOU TODAY?

### WHAT CAN YOU ASK CHRIST TO HELP YOU CARRY RIGHT NOW?

### WHAT IS YOUR HOPE FOR TOMORROW?

DATE    /    /

## Scripture of the Day

"Deny not the spirit of revelation, nor the spirit of prophecy, for wo unto him that denieth these things."

*Doctrine and Covenants 11:25*

## Quote of the Day

"Contrary to the doubts of some, there really *is* such a thing as right and wrong. There really *is* absolute truth—eternal truth. One of the plagues of our day is that too few people know where to turn for truth."

*Russell M. Nelson, "Pure Truth, Pure Doctrine, and Pure Revelation," October 2021*

### HOW DID GOD SHOW UP FOR YOU TODAY?

### WHAT CAN YOU ASK CHRIST TO HELP YOU CARRY RIGHT NOW?

### WHAT IS YOUR HOPE FOR TOMORROW?

DATE      /      /

## Scripture of the Day

*Articles of Faith 1:13*

"We believe in being honest, true, chaste, benevolent, virtuous, and in doing good to all men; indeed, we may say that we follow the admonition of Paul—We believe all things, we hope all things, we have endured many things, and hope to be able to endure all things. If there is anything virtuous, lovely, or of good report or praiseworthy, we seek after these things."

## Quote of the Day

*Ulisses Soares, "Followers of the Prince of Peace," April 2023*

"I promise you that as we pursue and develop these attributes, we will become more and more cordial and sensitive to the needs of our fellow beings and will experience joy, peace, and spiritual growth. Undoubtedly, the Lord will recognize our efforts and give us the gifts we need to be more tolerant and patient with one another's differences, weaknesses, and imperfections. Furthermore, we will be better able to resist the urge to take offense or offend those who hurt us. Our desire to forgive, as the Savior did, those who mistreat us or speak evil about us will surely increase and will become part of our character."

### HOW DID GOD SHOW UP FOR YOU TODAY?

### WHAT CAN YOU ASK CHRIST TO HELP YOU CARRY RIGHT NOW?

### WHAT IS YOUR HOPE FOR TOMORROW?

DATE     /     /

## Scripture of the Day

*Romans 8:26*

"Likewise the Spirit also helpeth our infirmities: for we know not what we should pray for as we ought: but the Spirit itself maketh intercession for us with groanings which cannot be uttered."

## Quote of the Day

*Amy A. Wright, "Christ Heals That Which Is Broken," April 2022*

"I spent countless hours at a cancer treatment facility, united in my suffering with many who were yearning to be healed. Some lived; others did not. I learned in a profound way that deliverance from our trials is different for each of us, and therefore our focus should be less about the *way* in which we are delivered and more about the Deliverer Himself. Our *emphasis* should always be on Jesus Christ!"

### HOW DID GOD SHOW UP FOR YOU TODAY?

### WHAT CAN YOU ASK CHRIST TO HELP YOU CARRY RIGHT NOW?

### WHAT IS YOUR HOPE FOR TOMORROW?

DATE     /     /

## Scripture of the Day

*Matthew 13:22–23*

"He also that received seed among the thorns is he that heareth the word; and the care of this world, and the deceitfulness of riches, choke the word, and he becometh unfruitful. But he that received seed into the good ground is he that heareth the word, and understandeth it; which also beareth fruit, and bringeth forth, some an hundredfold, some sixty, some thirty."

## Quote of the Day

*Vern P. Stanfill, "The Imperfect Harvest," April 2023*

"We must have the courage to believe that His grace is for us—that He will help us, rescue us from the depths when we falter, and perfect our less-than-perfect efforts."

### HOW DID GOD SHOW UP FOR YOU TODAY?

### WHAT CAN YOU ASK CHRIST TO HELP YOU CARRY RIGHT NOW?

### WHAT IS YOUR HOPE FOR TOMORROW?

DATE    /    /

## Scripture of the Day

*Mormon 9:21*

"Behold, I say unto you that whoso believeth in Christ, doubting nothing, whatsoever he shall ask the Father in the name of Christ it shall be granted him; and this promise is unto all, even unto the ends of the earth."

## Quote of the Day

*Alvin F. Meredith III, "Look down the Road," October 2021*

"While Peter kept his eyes focused on Jesus, he could walk on water. The storm, the waves, and the wind could not hinder him as long as he centered his focus on the Savior."

### HOW DID GOD SHOW UP FOR YOU TODAY?

### WHAT CAN YOU ASK CHRIST TO HELP YOU CARRY RIGHT NOW?

### WHAT IS YOUR HOPE FOR TOMORROW?

DATE    /    /

## Scripture of the Day

"What I the Lord have spoken, I have spoken, and I excuse not myself; and though the heavens and the earth pass away, my word shall not pass away, but shall all be fulfilled, whether by mine own voice or by the voice of my servants, it is the same."

*Doctrine and Covenants 1:38*

## Quote of the Day

"Some of you may feel you have fallen short in your efforts to follow the counsel of [the prophet]. If that is the case, then repent; begin again to follow the counsel of God's chosen prophet."

*Allen D. Haynie, "A Living Prophet for the Latter Days," April 2023*

### HOW DID GOD SHOW UP FOR YOU TODAY?

### WHAT CAN YOU ASK CHRIST TO HELP YOU CARRY RIGHT NOW?

### WHAT IS YOUR HOPE FOR TOMORROW?

DATE      /      /

## Scripture of the Day

"And I will bless them through thy name; for as many as receive this Gospel shall be called after thy name, and shall be accounted thy seed, and shall rise up and bless thee, as their father."

*Abraham 2:10*

## Quote of the Day

"Each of us has a divine potential because each is a child of God. Each is equal in His eyes. The implications of this truth are profound."

*Russell M. Nelson,
"Let God Prevail,"
October 2020*

### HOW DID GOD SHOW UP FOR YOU TODAY?

### WHAT CAN YOU ASK CHRIST TO HELP YOU CARRY RIGHT NOW?

### WHAT IS YOUR HOPE FOR TOMORROW?

DATE         /         /

## Scripture of the Day

*Isaiah 53:5*

"But he was wounded for our transgressions, he was bruised for our iniquities: the chastisement of our peace was upon him; and with his stripes we are healed."

## Quote of the Day

*Alvin F. Meredith III, "Look down the Road," October 2021*

"I believe that few things give the Savior more joy than saving those who turn, or return, to Him. The scriptures are full of stories of people who were once fallen and flawed but who repented and became firm in the faith of Christ. I think those stories are in the scriptures to remind us that the Savior's love for us and His power to redeem us are infinite. Not only does the Savior have joy when we repent, but we receive great joy as well."

### HOW DID GOD SHOW UP FOR YOU TODAY?

### WHAT CAN YOU ASK CHRIST TO HELP YOU CARRY RIGHT NOW?

### WHAT IS YOUR HOPE FOR TOMORROW?

DATE      /      /

## Scripture of the Day

*John 11:21, 32*

"Then said Martha unto Jesus, Lord, if thou hadst been here, my brother had not died. . . . Then when Mary was come where Jesus was, and saw him, she fell down at his feet, saying unto him, Lord, if thou hadst been here, my brother had not died."

## Quote of the Day

*W. Mark Bassett, "After the Fourth Day," April 2023*

"During our greatest worries, we, like Mary and Martha, seek the Savior or ask the Father for His divine intervention. The story of Lazarus teaches us principles that can be applied to our own lives as we face our individual challenges."

### HOW DID GOD SHOW UP FOR YOU TODAY?

### WHAT CAN YOU ASK CHRIST TO HELP YOU CARRY RIGHT NOW?

### WHAT IS YOUR HOPE FOR TOMORROW?

DATE  /  /

## Scripture of the Day

*2 Corinthians 4:17–18*

"For our light affliction, which is but for a moment, worketh for us a far more exceeding and eternal weight of glory; while we look not at the things which are seen, but at the things which are not seen: for the things which are seen are temporal; but the things which are not seen are eternal."

## Quote of the Day

*Russell M. Nelson, "Overcome the World and Find Rest," October 2022*

"Entering into a covenant relationship with God binds us to Him in a way that makes *everything* about life easier. Please do not misunderstand me: I did *not* say that making covenants makes life *easy*. In fact, expect opposition, because the adversary does not want you to discover the power of Jesus Christ. But yoking yourself with the Savior means you have access to *His* strength and redeeming power."

### HOW DID GOD SHOW UP FOR YOU TODAY?

### WHAT CAN YOU ASK CHRIST TO HELP YOU CARRY RIGHT NOW?

### WHAT IS YOUR HOPE FOR TOMORROW?

DATE      /      /

## Scripture of the Day

*1 Nephi 8:24*

"And it came to pass that I beheld others pressing forward, and they came forth and caught hold of the end of the rod of iron; and they did press forward through the mist of darkness, clinging to the rod of iron, even until they did come forth and partake of the fruit of the tree."

## Quote of the Day

*David A. Bednar, "But We Heeded Them Not," April 2022*

"I frankly do not have the ability to describe adequately the precise nature and power of our covenant connection with the resurrected and living Son of God. But I witness that the connections with Him and Heavenly Father are real and are the ultimate sources of assurance, peace, joy, and the spiritual strength that enable us to 'fear not, though the enemy deride.'"

### HOW DID GOD SHOW UP FOR YOU TODAY?

### WHAT CAN YOU ASK CHRIST TO HELP YOU CARRY RIGHT NOW?

### WHAT IS YOUR HOPE FOR TOMORROW?

DATE      /      /

## Scripture of the Day

*1 Nephi 15:8*

"Have ye inquired of the Lord?"

## Quote of the Day

*Henry B. Eyring, "The Faith to Ask and Then to Act," October 2021*

"The teenage Joseph Smith had faith sufficient to ask a question of God, believing that God would answer his heartfelt need. The answer that came changed the world. He wanted to know what church to join to be cleansed of sin. The answer he received encouraged him to keep asking ever-better questions and to act on the continuing flow of revelation that had just begun."

### HOW DID GOD SHOW UP FOR YOU TODAY?

### WHAT CAN YOU ASK CHRIST TO HELP YOU CARRY RIGHT NOW?

### WHAT IS YOUR HOPE FOR TOMORROW?

DATE         /         /

## *Scripture of the Day*

"I am the true light that lighteth every man that cometh into the world."

*Doctrine and Covenants 93:2*

## *Quote of the Day*

"Through Jesus Christ and His atoning sacrifice, we can experience a mighty change of mind and heart, bringing a fresh attitude, both toward God and toward life in general."

*Ulisses Soares, "Jesus Christ: The Caregiver of Our Soul," April 2021*

### HOW DID GOD SHOW UP FOR YOU TODAY?

### WHAT CAN YOU ASK CHRIST TO HELP YOU CARRY RIGHT NOW?

### WHAT IS YOUR HOPE FOR TOMORROW?

DATE  /  /

## Scripture of the Day

*Moses 6:59*

"That by reason of transgression cometh the fall, which fall bringeth death, and inasmuch as ye were born into the world by water, and blood, and the spirit, which I have made, and so became of dust a living soul, even so ye must be born again into the kingdom of heaven, of water, and of the Spirit, and be cleansed by blood, even the blood of mine Only Begotten; that ye might be sanctified from all sin, and enjoy the words of eternal life in this world, and eternal life in the world to come, even immortal glory."

## Quote of the Day

*Dale G. Renlund, "Consider the Goodness and Greatness of God," April 2020*

"When we consider the goodness of our Heavenly Father and Jesus Christ, our trust in Them increases. Our prayers change because we know God is our Father and we are His children. We seek not to change His will but to align our will with His and secure for ourselves blessings that He wants to grant, conditioned on our asking for them. We yearn to be more meek, more pure, more steadfast, more Christlike."

### HOW DID GOD SHOW UP FOR YOU TODAY?

### WHAT CAN YOU ASK CHRIST TO HELP YOU CARRY RIGHT NOW?

### WHAT IS YOUR HOPE FOR TOMORROW?

DATE    /    /

## Scripture of the Day

*Psalm 73:26*

"My flesh and my heart faileth: but God is the strength of my heart, and my portion for ever."

## Quote of the Day

*Dieter F. Uchtdorf, "God among Us," April 2021*

"My heart overflows with gratitude for my Heavenly Father. I realize that He has not doomed His children to stumble through mortality without hope for a bright and eternal future. He has provided instructions that reveal the way back to Him. And at the center of it all is *His Beloved Son, Jesus Christ*, and His sacrifice for us."

### HOW DID GOD SHOW UP FOR YOU TODAY?

### WHAT CAN YOU ASK CHRIST TO HELP YOU CARRY RIGHT NOW?

### WHAT IS YOUR HOPE FOR TOMORROW?

DATE    /    /

## *Scripture of the Day*

*1 John 4:19*

"We love him, because he first loved us."

## *Quote of the Day*

*Joy D. Jones, "Value beyond Measure," October 2017*

"Spiritual *worth* means to value ourselves the way Heavenly Father values us, not as the world values us. Our worth was determined before we ever came to this earth."

### HOW DID GOD SHOW UP FOR YOU TODAY?

### WHAT CAN YOU ASK CHRIST TO HELP YOU CARRY RIGHT NOW?

### WHAT IS YOUR HOPE FOR TOMORROW?

DATE        /        /

## Scripture of the Day

Mark 15:34

"And at the ninth hour Jesus cried with a loud voice, saying, Eloi, Eloi, lama sabachthani? which is, being interpreted, My God, my God, why hast thou forsaken me?"

## Quote of the Day

Dale G. Renlund, "Infuriating Unfairness," April 2021

"Jesus Christ both understands unfairness and has the power to provide a remedy. Nothing compares to the unfairness He endured. It was not fair that He experienced all the pains and afflictions of mankind. It was not fair that He suffered for my sins and mistakes and for yours. But He chose to do so because of His love for us and for Heavenly Father. He understands perfectly what we are experiencing."

### HOW DID GOD SHOW UP FOR YOU TODAY?

### WHAT CAN YOU ASK CHRIST TO HELP YOU CARRY RIGHT NOW?

### WHAT IS YOUR HOPE FOR TOMORROW?

DATE      /      /

## *Scripture of the Day*

*3 Nephi 4:10*

"But in this thing they were disappointed, for the Nephites did not fear them; but they did fear their God and did supplicate him for protection; therefore, when the armies of Giddianhi did rush upon them they were prepared to meet them; yea, in the strength of the Lord they did receive them."

## *Quote of the Day*

Bonnie H. Cordon, "Come unto Christ and Don't Come Alone," October 2021

"Have you ever had that searching feeling, wondering if Heavenly Father knows who you are and if He needs you? My dear youth, and to all, I testify the answer is *yes*! the Lord has a plan for you. He has prepared you for this day, *right now*, to be a strength and force for good in His mighty work. We need you! It simply will not be as grand without you!"

### HOW DID GOD SHOW UP FOR YOU TODAY?

### WHAT CAN YOU ASK CHRIST TO HELP YOU CARRY RIGHT NOW?

### WHAT IS YOUR HOPE FOR TOMORROW?

DATE     /     /

## Scripture of the Day

*2 Nephi 22:2*

"Behold, God is my salvation; I will trust, and not be afraid; for the Lord Jehovah is my strength and my song; he also has become my salvation."

## Quote of the Day

*Gerrit W. Gong, "Happy and Forever," October 2022*

"As we come to our Savior, we focus less on ourselves. We judge less and forgive more. Trusting His merits, mercy, and grace can free us from contention, anger, abuse, abandonment, unfairness, and the physical and mental challenges that sometimes come with a physical body in a mortal world."

### HOW DID GOD SHOW UP FOR YOU TODAY?

### WHAT CAN YOU ASK CHRIST TO HELP YOU CARRY RIGHT NOW?

### WHAT IS YOUR HOPE FOR TOMORROW?

DATE     /     /

## Scripture of the Day

*Doctrine and Covenants 58:4*

"For after much tribulation come the blessings. Wherefore the day cometh that ye shall be crowned with much glory; the hour is not yet, but is nigh at hand."

## Quote of the Day

*Dallin H. Oaks, "Be of Good Cheer," October 2020*

"Tribulation and challenges are the common experiences of mortality. Opposition is an essential part of the divine plan for helping us grow, and in the midst of that process, we have God's assurance that, in the long view of eternity, opposition will not be allowed to overcome us. With His help and our faithfulness and endurance, we will prevail. Like the mortal life of which they are a part, all tribulations are temporary."

### HOW DID GOD SHOW UP FOR YOU TODAY?

### WHAT CAN YOU ASK CHRIST TO HELP YOU CARRY RIGHT NOW?

### WHAT IS YOUR HOPE FOR TOMORROW?

DATE      /      /

### Scripture of the Day

*Abraham 3:22–23*

"Now the Lord had shown unto me, Abraham, the intelligences that were organized before the world was; and among all these there were many of the noble and great ones; and God saw these souls that they were good, and he stood in the midst of them, and he said: These I will make my rulers; for he stood among those that were spirits, and he saw that they were good; and he said unto me: Abraham, thou art one of them; thou wast chosen before thou wast born."

### Quote of the Day

*Randall K. Bennett, "Your Patriarchal Blessing—Inspired Direction from Heavenly Father," April 2023*

"Cherishing my patriarchal blessing while I was young blessed me with courage when I was discouraged, comfort when I was fearful, peace when I felt anxious, hope when I felt hopeless, and joy when I needed it most. My patriarchal blessing helped increase my faith and trust in my Heavenly Father and my Savior. It also increased my love for Them—and it still does."

#### HOW DID GOD SHOW UP FOR YOU TODAY?

#### WHAT CAN YOU ASK CHRIST TO HELP YOU CARRY RIGHT NOW?

#### WHAT IS YOUR HOPE FOR TOMORROW?

DATE        /        /

## Scripture of the Day

*Exodus 33:12–13*

"Thou hast said, I know thee by name, and thou hast also found grace in my sight. Now therefore, I pray thee, if I have found grace in thy sight, shew me now thy way, that I may know thee, that I may find grace in thy sight."

## Quote of the Day

*Reyna I. Aburto, "We Are The Church of Jesus Christ of Latter-day Saints," April 2022*

"My fellow disciples of Christ, let us not underestimate the marvelous work the Lord is doing through *us*, His Church, despite our shortcomings. Sometimes we are givers and sometimes we are receivers, but we are all one family in Christ. His Church is the structure He has given to guide and bless us as we worship Him and serve each other."

### HOW DID GOD SHOW UP FOR YOU TODAY?

### WHAT CAN YOU ASK CHRIST TO HELP YOU CARRY RIGHT NOW?

### WHAT IS YOUR HOPE FOR TOMORROW?

DATE      /      /

## Scripture of the Day

*Mark 10:21*

"Then Jesus beholding him loved him, and said unto him, One thing thou lackest: go thy way, sell whatsoever thou hast, and give to the poor, and thou shalt have treasure in heaven: and come, take up the cross, and follow me."

## Quote of the Day

*Jeffrey R. Holland, "The Greatest Possession," October 2021*

"When difficult things are asked of us, even things contrary to the longings of our heart, remember that the loyalty we pledge to the cause of Christ is to be the supreme devotion of our lives."

### HOW DID GOD SHOW UP FOR YOU TODAY?

### WHAT CAN YOU ASK CHRIST TO HELP YOU CARRY RIGHT NOW?

### WHAT IS YOUR HOPE FOR TOMORROW?

DATE    /    /

## Scripture of the Day

*Matthew 7:8*

"For every one that asketh receiveth; and he that seeketh findeth; and to him that knocketh it shall be opened."

## Quote of the Day

*Milton Camargo, "Ask, Seek, and Knock," October 2020*

"Why is revelation so essential to our spiritual survival? Because the world can be confusing and noisy, full of deception and distractions. Communication with our Father in Heaven enables us to sort through what is true and what is false, what is relevant to the Lord's plan for us and what is not. The world can also be harsh and heartbreaking. But as we open our hearts in prayer, we will feel the comfort that comes from our Father in Heaven and the assurance that He loves and values us."

### HOW DID GOD SHOW UP FOR YOU TODAY?

### WHAT CAN YOU ASK CHRIST TO HELP YOU CARRY RIGHT NOW?

### WHAT IS YOUR HOPE FOR TOMORROW?

DATE      /      /

## Scripture of the Day

"Whatsoever thing ye shall ask in faith, believing that ye shall receive in the name of Christ, ye shall receive it."

*Enos 1:15*

## Quote of the Day

"We can ask questions of our loving Heavenly Father, in the name of our merciful Savior, and the witness who answers our questions is the Holy Ghost, who always testifies of truth. Because the Holy Ghost works in perfect unity with Heavenly Father and Jesus Christ, we know that the manifestations of the Holy Ghost are reliable."

*Camille N. Johnson, "Invite Christ to Author Your Story," October 2021*

### HOW DID GOD SHOW UP FOR YOU TODAY?

### WHAT CAN YOU ASK CHRIST TO HELP YOU CARRY RIGHT NOW?

### WHAT IS YOUR HOPE FOR TOMORROW?

DATE    /    /

### Scripture of the Day

*Helaman 5:12*

"And now, my sons, remember, remember that it is upon the rock of our Redeemer, who is Christ, the Son of God, that ye must build your foundation; that when the devil shall send forth his mighty winds, yea, his shafts in the whirlwind, yea, when all his hail and his mighty storm shall beat upon you, it shall have no power over you to drag you down to the gulf of misery and endless wo, because of the rock upon which ye are built, which is a sure foundation, a foundation whereon if men build they cannot fall."

### Quote of the Day

*Evan A. Schmutz, "Trusting the Doctrine of Christ," April 2023*

"Jesus did not speak of the *possibility* of rain and flood and wind in our lives; He spoke of the *certainty* that storms will arise. The variable in this parable is not whether storms will come but how we have responded to His loving invitation to both hear and do what He has taught. There is no other way to survive."

#### HOW DID GOD SHOW UP FOR YOU TODAY?

#### WHAT CAN YOU ASK CHRIST TO HELP YOU CARRY RIGHT NOW?

#### WHAT IS YOUR HOPE FOR TOMORROW?

DATE    /    /

### Scripture of the Day

*Doctrine and Covenants 128:19*

"Now, what do we hear in the gospel which we have received? A voice of gladness! A voice of mercy from heaven; and a voice of truth out of the earth; glad tidings for the dead; a voice of gladness for the living and the dead; glad tidings of great joy."

### Quote of the Day

*Marcus B. Nash, "Hold Up Your Light," October 2021*

"When a person learns the glorious purpose of life, comes to understand that Christ forgives and succors those who follow Him, and then chooses to follow Christ into the waters of baptism, life changes for the better—even when the external circumstances of life do not."

#### HOW DID GOD SHOW UP FOR YOU TODAY?

#### WHAT CAN YOU ASK CHRIST TO HELP YOU CARRY RIGHT NOW?

#### WHAT IS YOUR HOPE FOR TOMORROW?

DATE    /    /

## Scripture of the Day

*Moses 7:32*

"The Lord said unto Enoch: Behold these thy brethren; they are the workmanship of mine own hands, and I gave unto them their knowledge, in the day I created them; and in the Garden of Eden, gave I unto man his agency."

## Quote of the Day

*Dale G. Renlund, "Accessing God's Power through Covenants," April 2023*

"We can choose whether we yield to heavenly powers or 'go with the flow.' Going against the flow may be difficult. But when we yield 'to the enticings of the Holy Spirit' and put off the selfish tendencies of the natural man or woman, we can receive the Savior's transforming power in our lives, the power to do difficult things."

### HOW DID GOD SHOW UP FOR YOU TODAY?

### WHAT CAN YOU ASK CHRIST TO HELP YOU CARRY RIGHT NOW?

### WHAT IS YOUR HOPE FOR TOMORROW?

DATE    /    /

## *Scripture of the Day*

"And ye shall seek me, and find me, when ye shall search for me with all your heart."

*Jeremiah 29:13*

## *Quote of the Day*

"We cannot lose our love for and hope in Jesus, even if we face seemingly overwhelming challenges. Heavenly Father and Jesus will never forget us. They love us."

*M. Russell Ballard,*
*"Lovest Thou Me*
*More Than These?"*
*October 2021*

### HOW DID GOD SHOW UP FOR YOU TODAY?

### WHAT CAN YOU ASK CHRIST TO HELP YOU CARRY RIGHT NOW?

### WHAT IS YOUR HOPE FOR TOMORROW?

DATE      /      /

**Scripture of the Day**

*James 1:22*

"But be ye doers of the word, and not hearers only, deceiving your own selves."

**Quote of the Day**

*Bonnie H. Cordon, "Never Give Up an Opportunity to Testify of Christ," April 2023*

"I have attended the temple many times, but when I *worship in the house of the Lord*, it changes me. Sometimes while fasting, I find myself simply going hungry, but other times, I *feast on the Spirit with purpose*. I sometimes have mumbled prayers that are repetitive and routine, but I have also come *eager to receive counsel from the Lord through prayer*. There is power in making these holy habits less of a checklist and more of a witness."

### HOW DID GOD SHOW UP FOR YOU TODAY?

### WHAT CAN YOU ASK CHRIST TO HELP YOU CARRY RIGHT NOW?

### WHAT IS YOUR HOPE FOR TOMORROW?

DATE    /    /

**Scripture of the Day**

*John 14:21*

"He that hath my commandments, and keepeth them, he it is that loveth me: and he that loveth me shall be loved of my Father, and I will love him, and will manifest myself to him."

**Quote of the Day**

*D. Todd Christofferson, "The Love of God," October 2021*

"This divine love should give us abundant comfort and confidence as we pray to the Father in the name of Christ. Not one of us is a stranger to Them. We need not hesitate to call upon God, even when we feel unworthy. We can rely on the mercy and merits of Jesus Christ to be heard. As we abide in God's love, we depend less and less on the approval of others to guide us."

### HOW DID GOD SHOW UP FOR YOU TODAY?

### WHAT CAN YOU ASK CHRIST TO HELP YOU CARRY RIGHT NOW?

### WHAT IS YOUR HOPE FOR TOMORROW?

DATE     /     /

## Scripture of the Day

*Alma 33:22*

"Cast about your eyes and begin to believe in the Son of God, that he will come to redeem his people, and that he shall suffer and die to atone for their sins; and that he shall rise again from the dead, which shall bring to pass the resurrection, that all men shall stand before him, to be judged at the last and judgment day, according to their works."

## Quote of the Day

*Anthony D. Perkins, "Remember Thy Suffering Saints, O Our God," October 2021*

"Jesus Christ offers His enabling power to help you have strength to endure your suffering well. This enabling power is made possible through His Atonement. I fear that too many Church members think if they are just a little tougher, they can get through any suffering on their own. This is a hard way to live. Your temporary moment of strength can never compare to the Savior's infinite supply of power to fortify your soul."

### HOW DID GOD SHOW UP FOR YOU TODAY?

### WHAT CAN YOU ASK CHRIST TO HELP YOU CARRY RIGHT NOW?

### WHAT IS YOUR HOPE FOR TOMORROW?

DATE     /     /

## Scripture of the Day

*1 Nephi 17:3*

"And thus we see that the commandments of God must be fulfilled. And if it so be that the children of men keep the commandments of God he doth nourish them, and strengthen them, and provide means whereby they can accomplish the thing which he has commanded them; wherefore, he did provide means for us while we did sojourn in the wilderness."

## Quote of the Day

*Jean B. Bingham, "Covenants with God Strengthen, Protect, and Prepare Us for Eternal Glory," April 2022*

"Life's experiences can range from humorous to heart-wrenching, from grim to glorious. Each experience helps us understand more about our Father's encompassing love and our capacity to change through the Savior's gift of grace. Keeping our covenants allows the Savior's power to cleanse us as we learn through experience—whether it is a minor misjudgment or a major failing. Our Redeemer is there to catch us when we fall *if* we turn to Him."

### HOW DID GOD SHOW UP FOR YOU TODAY?

### WHAT CAN YOU ASK CHRIST TO HELP YOU CARRY RIGHT NOW?

### WHAT IS YOUR HOPE FOR TOMORROW?

DATE    /    /

## Scripture of the Day

*Doctrine and Covenants 124:39*

"Therefore, verily I say unto you, that your anointings, and your washings, and your baptisms for the dead, and your solemn assemblies, and your memorials for your sacrifices by the sons of Levi, and for your oracles in your most holy places wherein you receive conversations, and your statutes and judgments, for the beginning of the revelations and foundation of Zion, and for the glory, honor, and endowment of all her municipals, are ordained by the ordinance of my holy house, which my people are always commanded to build unto my holy name."

## Quote of the Day

*Kevin R. Duncan, "A Voice of Gladness!" April 2023*

"As members of the Church today, some of us may find it easy to take these glorious eternal truths for granted. They have become second nature to us. Sometimes it is helpful when we see them through the eyes of those who learn about them for the very first time."

### HOW DID GOD SHOW UP FOR YOU TODAY?

### WHAT CAN YOU ASK CHRIST TO HELP YOU CARRY RIGHT NOW?

### WHAT IS YOUR HOPE FOR TOMORROW?

DATE      /      /

**Scripture of the Day**

"For behold, this is my work and my glory—to bring to pass the immortality and eternal life of man."

*Moses 1:39*

**Quote of the Day**

"We lift our voices in praise of our bountiful and forgiving God. For surely He is a God of new beginnings. The sublime end of all His labor is to help us, His children, succeed in our quest for immortality and eternal life."

*Dieter F. Uchtdorf, "Daily Restoration," October 2021*

### HOW DID GOD SHOW UP FOR YOU TODAY?

### WHAT CAN YOU ASK CHRIST TO HELP YOU CARRY RIGHT NOW?

### WHAT IS YOUR HOPE FOR TOMORROW?

DATE      /      /

**Scripture of the Day**

*Psalm 46:10*

"Be still, and know that I am God: I will be exalted among the heathen, I will be exalted in the earth."

**Quote of the Day**

*Russell M. Nelson, "Let Your Faith Show," April 2014*

"Faith is the antidote for fear."

### HOW DID GOD SHOW UP FOR YOU TODAY?

### WHAT CAN YOU ASK CHRIST TO HELP YOU CARRY RIGHT NOW?

### WHAT IS YOUR HOPE FOR TOMORROW?

DATE    /    /

## Scripture of the Day

---

*John 15:10*

"If ye keep my commandments, ye shall abide in my love; even as I have kept my Father's commandments, and abide in his love."

## Quote of the Day

---

*David A. Bednar, "Abide in Me, and I in You; Therefore Walk with Me," April 2023*

"We begin to abide in the Lord by exercising our moral agency to take upon ourselves His yoke through the covenants and ordinances of the restored gospel. The covenant connection we have with our Heavenly Father and His resurrected and living Son is the supernal source of perspective, hope, power, peace, and enduring joy; it also is the rock-solid foundation upon which we should build our lives."

### HOW DID GOD SHOW UP FOR YOU TODAY?

### WHAT CAN YOU ASK CHRIST TO HELP YOU CARRY RIGHT NOW?

### WHAT IS YOUR HOPE FOR TOMORROW?

DATE    /    /

## Scripture of the Day

*2 Corinthians 12:9–10*

"Most gladly therefore will I rather glory in my infirmities, that the power of Christ may rest upon me. . . . for when I am weak, then am I strong."

## Quote of the Day

*M. Russell Ballard, "Follow Jesus Christ with Footsteps of Faith," October 2022*

"There is hope in the Lord Jesus Christ. There is hope for all in this life. There is hope to overcome our mistakes, our sorrows, our struggles, and our trials and our troubles. There is hope in repentance and being forgiven and in forgiving others. I testify that there is hope and peace in Christ. He can carry us today through difficult times. He did it for the early pioneers, and He will do it now for each one of us."

### HOW DID GOD SHOW UP FOR YOU TODAY?

### WHAT CAN YOU ASK CHRIST TO HELP YOU CARRY RIGHT NOW?

### WHAT IS YOUR HOPE FOR TOMORROW?

DATE    /    /

## Scripture of the Day

*Moroni 7:26*

"Whatsoever thing ye shall ask the Father in my name, which is good, in faith believing that ye shall receive, behold, it shall be done unto you."

## Quote of the Day

*Chi Hong (Sam) Wong, "They Cannot Prevail; We Cannot Fall," April 2021*

"God is our Heavenly Father. He loves all of us. He knows our potential way better than we know ourselves. He knows not only the details of our lives. God knows the details of the details of the details of our lives."

### HOW DID GOD SHOW UP FOR YOU TODAY?

### WHAT CAN YOU ASK CHRIST TO HELP YOU CARRY RIGHT NOW?

### WHAT IS YOUR HOPE FOR TOMORROW?

DATE    /    /

## Scripture of the Day

"And I will tell you of the wrestle which I had before God, before I received a remission of my sins."

*Enos 1:2*

## Quote of the Day

"Everything good in life—every potential blessing of eternal significance—begins with faith. Allowing God to prevail in our lives begins with faith that He is willing to guide us. True repentance begins with faith that Jesus Christ has the power to cleanse, heal, and strengthen us."

*Russell M. Nelson, "Christ Is Risen; Faith in Him Will Move Mountains," April 2021*

### HOW DID GOD SHOW UP FOR YOU TODAY?

### WHAT CAN YOU ASK CHRIST TO HELP YOU CARRY RIGHT NOW?

### WHAT IS YOUR HOPE FOR TOMORROW?

DATE    /    /

## Scripture of the Day

*Doctrine and Covenants 21:5*

"For his word ye shall receive, as if from mine own mouth, in all patience and faith."

## Quote of the Day

*Allen D. Haynie, "A Living Prophet for the Latter Days," April 2023*

"Even if you are unsure, I witness that we can withstand the heat of the latter days and even thrive in them. We are the Saints of the latter days, and these are great days. We were anxious to come to the earth at this time, having confidence that we would not be left to stumble when confronted by the adversary's increasingly darker and more confusing mists but rather to take counsel and direction from he who is authorized to say to us and the entire world, 'Thus saith the Lord God.'"

### HOW DID GOD SHOW UP FOR YOU TODAY?

### WHAT CAN YOU ASK CHRIST TO HELP YOU CARRY RIGHT NOW?

### WHAT IS YOUR HOPE FOR TOMORROW?

DATE    /    /

## Scripture of the Day

*Moses 6:32, 34*

"And the Lord said unto Enoch: Go forth and do as I have commanded thee, and no man shall pierce thee. Open thy mouth, and it shall be filled, and I will give thee utterance, for all flesh is in my hands, and I will do as seemeth me good. . . . Behold my Spirit is upon you, wherefore all thy words will I justify; and the mountains shall flee before you, and the rivers shall turn from their course; and thou shalt abide in me, and I in you; therefore walk with me."

## Quote of the Day

*David A. Bednar, "Abide in Me, and I in You; Therefore Walk with Me," April 2023*

"Enoch ultimately became a mighty prophet and a tool in God's hands to accomplish a great work, but he did not start his ministry that way! Rather, his capacity over time was magnified as he learned to abide in and walk with the Son of God."

### HOW DID GOD SHOW UP FOR YOU TODAY?

### WHAT CAN YOU ASK CHRIST TO HELP YOU CARRY RIGHT NOW?

### WHAT IS YOUR HOPE FOR TOMORROW?

DATE        /        /

**Scripture of the Day**

*Psalm 147:3*

"He healeth the broken in heart, and bindeth up their wounds."

**Quote of the Day**

*Anthony D. Perkins, "Remember Thy Suffering Saints, O Our God," October 2021*

"Heavenly Father is intimately aware of your suffering. While in the midst of trials, we can mistakenly think that God is far away and unconcerned with our pain. Even the Prophet Joseph Smith expressed this feeling at a low point in his life. . . . The Lord's answer reassured Joseph and all who suffer."

HOW DID GOD SHOW UP FOR YOU TODAY?

WHAT CAN YOU ASK CHRIST TO HELP YOU CARRY RIGHT NOW?

WHAT IS YOUR HOPE FOR TOMORROW?

DATE     /     /

## *Scripture of the Day*

"But the Comforter, which is the Holy Ghost, whom the Father will send in my name, he shall teach you all things, and bring all things to your remembrance, whatsoever I have said unto you."

*John 14:26*

## *Quote of the Day*

"While we may not enjoy the same physical proximity as those who walked with Christ during His earthly ministry, through the Holy Ghost we can experience His power every day! As much as we need!"

*Bonnie H. Cordon, "Never Give Up an Opportunity to Testify of Christ," April 2023*

### HOW DID GOD SHOW UP FOR YOU TODAY?

### WHAT CAN YOU ASK CHRIST TO HELP YOU CARRY RIGHT NOW?

### WHAT IS YOUR HOPE FOR TOMORROW?

DATE    /    /

## Scripture of the Day

*Matthew 5:48*

"Be ye therefore perfect, even as your Father which is in heaven is perfect."

## Quote of the Day

*Vern P. Stanfill, "The Imperfect Harvest," April 2023*

"As we accept the Savior's invitation to come unto Him, we soon realize that our best is good enough and that the grace of a loving Savior will make up the difference in ways we cannot imagine."

### HOW DID GOD SHOW UP FOR YOU TODAY?

### WHAT CAN YOU ASK CHRIST TO HELP YOU CARRY RIGHT NOW?

### WHAT IS YOUR HOPE FOR TOMORROW?

DATE      /      /

**Scripture of the Day**

*Omni 1:26*

"Come unto Christ, who is the Holy One of Israel, and partake of his salvation, and the power of his redemption. Yea, come unto him, and offer your whole souls as an offering unto him, and continue in fasting and praying, and endure to the end; and as the Lord liveth ye will be saved."

**Quote of the Day**

*Amy A. Wright, "Christ Heals That Which Is Broken," April 2022*

"Because of Christ, our decision to 'go forth and change' can also allow us to 'go forth and heal,' for He is the source of healing all that is broken in our lives. As the great Mediator and Advocate with the Father, Christ sanctifies and restores broken relationships—most important, our relationship with God."

### HOW DID GOD SHOW UP FOR YOU TODAY?

### WHAT CAN YOU ASK CHRIST TO HELP YOU CARRY RIGHT NOW?

### WHAT IS YOUR HOPE FOR TOMORROW?

DATE    /    /

## Scripture of the Day

*Mormon 9:15*

"And now, O all ye that have imagined up unto yourselves a god who can do no miracles, I would ask of you, have all these things passed, of which I have spoken? Has the end come yet? Behold I say unto you, Nay; and God has not ceased to be a God of miracles."

## Quote of the Day

*Vaiangina Sikahema, "A House of Sequential Order," October 2021*

"Miracles operate according to sequential order. Miracles occur when we first exercise faith. Faith precedes the miracle."

### HOW DID GOD SHOW UP FOR YOU TODAY?

### WHAT CAN YOU ASK CHRIST TO HELP YOU CARRY RIGHT NOW?

### WHAT IS YOUR HOPE FOR TOMORROW?

DATE / /

## *Scripture of the Day*

*Doctrine and Covenants 6:23*

"Did I not speak peace to your mind concerning the matter? What greater witness can you have than from God?"

## *Quote of the Day*

*Arnulfo Valenzuela, "Deepening Our Conversion to Jesus Christ," October 2021*

"The Holy Ghost guides us toward truth and testifies to us of the truth. He illuminates our minds and renews our understanding and touches our hearts through God's revelation, the source of all truth. The Holy Ghost purifies our hearts. He inspires in us the desire to live according to the truth and whispers to us ways to do so."

### HOW DID GOD SHOW UP FOR YOU TODAY?

### WHAT CAN YOU ASK CHRIST TO HELP YOU CARRY RIGHT NOW?

### WHAT IS YOUR HOPE FOR TOMORROW?

DATE     /     /

## Scripture of the Day

*Moroni 10:32*

"Yea, come unto Christ, and be perfected in him, and deny yourselves of all ungodliness; and if ye shall deny yourselves of all ungodliness, and love God with all your might, mind and strength, then is his grace sufficient for you, that by his grace ye may be perfect in Christ; and if by the grace of God ye are perfect in Christ, ye can in nowise deny the power of God."

## Quote of the Day

*Dale G. Renlund, "Accessing God's Power through Covenants," April 2023*

"As you come to Christ and are connected to Him and our Heavenly Father by covenant, something seemingly unnatural happens. You are transformed and become perfected in Jesus Christ. You become a covenant child of God and an inheritor in His kingdom. I can imagine Him saying to you, 'Thou art my dear child in whom I delight. Welcome home.'"

### HOW DID GOD SHOW UP FOR YOU TODAY?

### WHAT CAN YOU ASK CHRIST TO HELP YOU CARRY RIGHT NOW?

### WHAT IS YOUR HOPE FOR TOMORROW?

DATE        /        /

## Scripture of the Day

1 Samuel 17:37

"David said moreover, The Lord that delivered me out of the paw of the lion, and out of the paw of the bear, he will deliver me out of the hand of this Philistine. And Saul said unto David, Go, and the Lord be with thee."

## Quote of the Day

Camille N. Johnson,
"Invite Christ to Author Your Story,"
October 2021

"Why do we want the Savior to be the author and the finisher of our stories? Because He knows our potential perfectly, He will take us to places we never imagined ourselves. He may make us a David or an Esther. He will stretch us and refine us to be more like Him. The things we will achieve as we act with more faith will increase our faith in Jesus Christ."

### HOW DID GOD SHOW UP FOR YOU TODAY?

### WHAT CAN YOU ASK CHRIST TO HELP YOU CARRY RIGHT NOW?

### WHAT IS YOUR HOPE FOR TOMORROW?

DATE      /      /

## Scripture of the Day

*Galatians 3:27–28*

"For as many of you as have been baptized into Christ have put on Christ. There is neither Jew nor Greek, there is neither bond nor free, there is neither male nor female: for ye are all one in Christ Jesus."

## Quote of the Day

*D. Todd Christofferson, "One in Christ," April 2023*

"We are too diverse and at times too discordant to be able to come together as one on any other basis or under any other name. Only in Jesus Christ can we truly become one. Becoming one in Christ happens one by one—we each begin with ourselves."

### HOW DID GOD SHOW UP FOR YOU TODAY?

### WHAT CAN YOU ASK CHRIST TO HELP YOU CARRY RIGHT NOW?

### WHAT IS YOUR HOPE FOR TOMORROW?

DATE    /    /

## Scripture of the Day

*1 John 2:3–6*

"And hereby we do know that we know him, if we keep his commandments. He that saith, I know him, and keepeth not his commandments, is a liar, and the truth is not in him. But whoso keepeth his word, in him verily is the love of God perfected: hereby know we that we are in him. He that saith he abideth in him ought himself also so to walk, even as he walked."

## Quote of the Day

*Ulisses Soares, "The Savior's Abiding Compassion," October 2021*

"Compassion is a fundamental characteristic of those who strive for sanctification, and this divine quality intertwines with other Christian traits such as mourning with those who mourn and having empathy, mercy, and kindness. The expression of compassion for others is, in fact, the essence of the gospel of Jesus Christ and a marked evidence of our spiritual and emotional closeness to the Savior. Furthermore, it shows the level of influence He has on our way of life and demonstrates the magnitude of our spirits."

### HOW DID GOD SHOW UP FOR YOU TODAY?

### WHAT CAN YOU ASK CHRIST TO HELP YOU CARRY RIGHT NOW?

### WHAT IS YOUR HOPE FOR TOMORROW?

DATE      /      /

## Scripture of the Day

*Mosiah 5:2*

"We believe all the words which thou hast spoken unto us; and also, we know of their surety and truth, because of the Spirit of the Lord Omnipotent, which has wrought a mighty change in us, or in our hearts, that we have no more disposition to do evil, but to do good continually."

## Quote of the Day

*Becky Craven, "Keep the Change," October 2020*

"He gives us much, much more than the value of what we can ever return to Him. So, what can we give to Him, who paid the incalculable price for our sins? We can give Him *change*. We can give Him our *change*. It may be a change of thought, a change in habit, or a change in the direction we are headed. In return for His priceless payment for each of us, the Lord asks us for a change of heart. The change He requests from us is not for His benefit but for ours. So, unlike the purchaser at the market who would take back the change we offer, our gracious Savior beckons us to *keep the change.*"

### HOW DID GOD SHOW UP FOR YOU TODAY?

### WHAT CAN YOU ASK CHRIST TO HELP YOU CARRY RIGHT NOW?

### WHAT IS YOUR HOPE FOR TOMORROW?

DATE    /    /

## Scripture of the Day

*1 Nephi 13:37*

"And blessed are they who shall seek to bring forth my Zion at that day, for they shall have the gift and the power of the Holy Ghost; and if they endure unto the end they shall be lifted up at the last day, and shall be saved in the everlasting kingdom of the Lamb; and whoso shall publish peace, yea, tidings of great joy, how beautiful upon the mountains shall they be."

## Quote of the Day

*Neil L. Andersen, "Following Jesus: Being a Peacemaker," April 2022*

"How does a peacemaker calm and cool the fiery darts? Certainly not by shrinking before those who disparage us. Rather, we remain confident in our faith, sharing our beliefs with conviction but always void of anger or malice."

### HOW DID GOD SHOW UP FOR YOU TODAY?

### WHAT CAN YOU ASK CHRIST TO HELP YOU CARRY RIGHT NOW?

### WHAT IS YOUR HOPE FOR TOMORROW?

**DATE**  /  /

## *Scripture of the Day*

*Doctrine and Covenants 18:10*

"Remember the worth of souls is great in the sight of God."

## *Quote of the Day*

*Dieter F. Uchtdorf, "Jesus Christ Is the Strength of Youth," October 2022*

"If the Savior were here right now, what would He say to you? I believe He would start by expressing His deep love for you. He might say it with words, but it would also flow so strongly—just from His presence—that it would be unmistakable, reaching deep into your heart, filling your whole soul!"

### HOW DID GOD SHOW UP FOR YOU TODAY?

### WHAT CAN YOU ASK CHRIST TO HELP YOU CARRY RIGHT NOW?

### WHAT IS YOUR HOPE FOR TOMORROW?

DATE     /     /

## Scripture of the Day

"He knoweth the way that I take: when he hath tried me, I shall come forth as gold."

*Job 23:10*

## Quote of the Day

"You are a cherished, beloved child of Heavenly Father. He loves you so perfectly that He sent His Son, Jesus Christ, to atone for you and for me. The Savior's love for us is unfailing—even when we fail!"

*Bonnie H. Cordon, "Come unto Christ and Don't Come Alone," October 2021*

### HOW DID GOD SHOW UP FOR YOU TODAY?

### WHAT CAN YOU ASK CHRIST TO HELP YOU CARRY RIGHT NOW?

### WHAT IS YOUR HOPE FOR TOMORROW?

DATE    /    /

## Scripture of the Day

Matthew 11:29–30

"Take my yoke upon you, and learn of me; for I am meek and lowly in heart: and ye shall find rest unto your souls. For my yoke is easy, and my burden is light."

## Quote of the Day

Camille N. Johnson, "Jesus Christ Is Relief," April 2023

"That the yoke is easy and the burden is light presumes we get in the yoke with the Savior, that we share our burdens with Him, that we let Him lift our load. That means entering into a covenant relationship with God and keeping that covenant, which . . . 'makes *everything* about life easier.'"

### HOW DID GOD SHOW UP FOR YOU TODAY?

### WHAT CAN YOU ASK CHRIST TO HELP YOU CARRY RIGHT NOW?

### WHAT IS YOUR HOPE FOR TOMORROW?

DATE      /      /

## Scripture of the Day

*1 Corinthians 15:57*

"But thanks be to God, which giveth us the victory through our Lord Jesus Christ."

## Quote of the Day

*Tracy Y. Browning, "Seeing More of Jesus Christ in Our Lives," October 2022*

"Friends, Jesus Christ is both the purpose of our focus and the intent of our destination. To help us to remain fixed and heading in the right direction, the Savior invites us to see our lives *through Him* in order to see *more of Him* in our lives."

### HOW DID GOD SHOW UP FOR YOU TODAY?

### WHAT CAN YOU ASK CHRIST TO HELP YOU CARRY RIGHT NOW?

### WHAT IS YOUR HOPE FOR TOMORROW?

DATE  /  /

## Scripture of the Day

*Alma 27:18*

"Now was not this exceeding joy? Behold, this is joy which none receiveth save it be the truly penitent and humble seeker of happiness."

## Quote of the Day

*Anthony D. Perkins, "Remember Thy Suffering Saints, O Lord," October 2021*

"Choose to find joy each day. Those who suffer often feel that the night just goes on and on, and daylight will never come. It is OK to weep. Yet, if you find yourself in dark nights of suffering, by choosing faith you can awake to bright mornings of rejoicing."

### HOW DID GOD SHOW UP FOR YOU TODAY?

### WHAT CAN YOU ASK CHRIST TO HELP YOU CARRY RIGHT NOW?

### WHAT IS YOUR HOPE FOR TOMORROW?

DATE    /    /

## Scripture of the Day

*3 Nephi 17:9*

"And it came to pass that when he had thus spoken, all the multitude, with one accord, did go forth with their sick and their afflicted, and their lame, and with their blind, and with their dumb, and with all them that were afflicted in any manner; and he did heal them every one as they were brought forth unto him."

## Quote of the Day

*Ulisses Soares, "The Savior's Abiding Compassion," October 2021*

"It is meaningful to observe that Jesus's compassionate acts were not occasional or mandated manifestations based on a list of tasks to be completed but everyday expressions of the reality of His pure love for God and His children and His abiding desire to help them."

### HOW DID GOD SHOW UP FOR YOU TODAY?

### WHAT CAN YOU ASK CHRIST TO HELP YOU CARRY RIGHT NOW?

### WHAT IS YOUR HOPE FOR TOMORROW?

DATE    /    /

## *Scripture of the Day*

*Doctrine and Covenants 6:36*

"Look unto me in every thought; doubt not, fear not."

## *Quote of the Day*

*Alvin F. Meredith III, "Look down the Road," October 2021*

"Focusing on Christ requires discipline, especially about the small and simple spiritual habits that help us become better disciples. There is no discipleship without discipline. Our focus on Christ becomes more clear when we look down the road at where we want to be and who we want to become and then make time every day to do those things that will help us get there. Focusing on Christ can simplify our decisions and provide a guide for how we can best spend our time and resources."

### HOW DID GOD SHOW UP FOR YOU TODAY?

### WHAT CAN YOU ASK CHRIST TO HELP YOU CARRY RIGHT NOW?

### WHAT IS YOUR HOPE FOR TOMORROW?

DATE    /    /

**Scripture of the Day**

*Malachi 4:5–6*

"Behold, I will send you Elijah the prophet before the coming of the great and dreadful day of the Lord: And he shall turn the heart of the fathers to the children, and the heart of the children to their fathers, lest I come and smite the earth with a curse."

**Quote of the Day**

*Benjamín De Hoyos, "The Work of the Temple and Family History— One and the Same Work," April 2023*

"But let us remember that family history is more than just looking for names, dates, and places. It is uniting families and feeling the joy that comes from extending to them the ordinances of the gospel."

### HOW DID GOD SHOW UP FOR YOU TODAY?

### WHAT CAN YOU ASK CHRIST TO HELP YOU CARRY RIGHT NOW?

### WHAT IS YOUR HOPE FOR TOMORROW?

DATE    /    /

## *Scripture of the Day*

"Now the God of hope fill you with all joy and peace in believing, that ye may abound in hope, through the power of the Holy Ghost."

*Romans 15:13*

## *Quote of the Day*

"In the scriptures, the word *joy* typically means much more than passing moments of contentment or even feelings of happiness. Joy in this context is a godly attribute, found in its fulness when we return to dwell in the presence of God. It is more profound, elevating, enduring, and lifechanging than any pleasure or comfort this world can offer."

*Craig C. Christensen, "There Can Be Nothing So Exquisite and Sweet as Was My Joy," April 2023*

### HOW DID GOD SHOW UP FOR YOU TODAY?

### WHAT CAN YOU ASK CHRIST TO HELP YOU CARRY RIGHT NOW?

### WHAT IS YOUR HOPE FOR TOMORROW?

DATE    /    /

## Scripture of the Day

"Verily, verily, I say unto you, He that believeth on me, the works that I do shall he do also; and greater works than these shall he do; because I go unto my Father."

*John 14:12*

## Quote of the Day

"The Savior stands ready to accept our humble offerings and perfect them through His grace. With Christ, there is no imperfect harvest."

*Vern P. Stanfill, "The Imperfect Harvest," April 2023*

### HOW DID GOD SHOW UP FOR YOU TODAY?

### WHAT CAN YOU ASK CHRIST TO HELP YOU CARRY RIGHT NOW?

### WHAT IS YOUR HOPE FOR TOMORROW?

DATE        /        /

## Scripture of the Day

2 Nephi 27:23

"For behold, I am God; and I am a God of miracles; and I will show unto the world that I am the same yesterday, today, and forever; and I work not among the children of men save it be according to their faith."

## Quote of the Day

Bradley R. Wilcox, "Worthiness Is Not Flawlessness," October 2021

"Some mistakenly receive the message that they are not worthy to participate fully in the gospel because they are not completely free of bad habits. God's message is that worthiness is not flawlessness. Worthiness is being honest and trying. We must be honest with God, priesthood leaders, and others who love us, and we must strive to keep God's commandments and never give up just because we slip up."

### HOW DID GOD SHOW UP FOR YOU TODAY?

### WHAT CAN YOU ASK CHRIST TO HELP YOU CARRY RIGHT NOW?

### WHAT IS YOUR HOPE FOR TOMORROW?

DATE    /    /

## Scripture of the Day

"I prayed unto the Lord; and after I had prayed the winds did cease, and the storm did cease, and there was a great calm."

*1 Nephi 18:21*

## Quote of the Day

"Jesus Christ is the light that we should hold up even during the dark times of our mortal life. When we choose to follow Christ, we choose to be changed. A man or woman changed for Christ will be captained by Christ."

*Thierry K. Mutombo, "Ye Shall Be Free," April 2021*

### HOW DID GOD SHOW UP FOR YOU TODAY?

### WHAT CAN YOU ASK CHRIST TO HELP YOU CARRY RIGHT NOW?

### WHAT IS YOUR HOPE FOR TOMORROW?

DATE     /     /

**Scripture of the Day**

*Doctrine and Covenants 138:55–56*

"I observed that they were also among the noble and great ones who were chosen in the beginning to be rulers in the Church of God. Even before they were born, they, with many others, received their first lessons in the world of spirits and were prepared to come forth in the due time of the Lord to labor in his vineyard for the salvation of the souls of men."

**Quote of the Day**

*Benjamín De Hoyos, "The Work of the Temple and Family History— One and the Same Work," April 2023*

"As we follow the guidance of the prophets and learn how to do our family history and perform the temple ordinances for our ancestors, we will experience great joy to the point that we will not want to stop doing it. The Spirit will flood our hearts, awaken our faculties to do it, and guide us as we search for the names of our ancestors."

HOW DID GOD SHOW UP FOR YOU TODAY?

WHAT CAN YOU ASK CHRIST TO HELP YOU CARRY RIGHT NOW?

WHAT IS YOUR HOPE FOR TOMORROW?

DATE     /     /

**Scripture of the Day**

For I know that my redeemer liveth, and that he shall stand at the latter day upon the earth."

*Job 19:25*

**Quote of the Day**

"The God of heaven and earth will help us overcome discouragement and whatever obstacles we encounter if we look to Him, follow the promptings of the Holy Ghost, and just keep going—with faith."

*Carl B. Cook, "Just Keep Going—with Faith," April 2023*

### HOW DID GOD SHOW UP FOR YOU TODAY?

### WHAT CAN YOU ASK CHRIST TO HELP YOU CARRY RIGHT NOW?

### WHAT IS YOUR HOPE FOR TOMORROW?

DATE      /     /

## Scripture of the Day

*Matthew 7:21*

"Not every one that saith unto me, Lord, Lord, shall enter into the kingdom of heaven; but he that doeth the will of my Father which is in heaven."

## Quote of the Day

*Dale G. Renlund, "Accessing God's Power through Covenants," April 2023*

"We become His disciples and represent Him well when we intentionally and incrementally take on ourselves the name of Jesus Christ through covenants. Our covenants give us power to stay on the covenant path because our relationship with Jesus Christ and our Heavenly Father is changed. We are connected to Them by a covenantal bond."

### HOW DID GOD SHOW UP FOR YOU TODAY?

### WHAT CAN YOU ASK CHRIST TO HELP YOU CARRY RIGHT NOW?

### WHAT IS YOUR HOPE FOR TOMORROW?

DATE     /     /

## Scripture of the Day

*John 14:1*

"Let not your heart be troubled: ye believe in God, believe also in me."

## Quote of the Day

*Ulisses Soares, "Jesus Christ: The Caregiver of Our Soul," April 2021*

"I assure you that as we put our trust in Jesus Christ and in His supernal atoning sacrifice, enduring in our faith to the end, we will enjoy the promises of our beloved Heavenly Father, who does everything within His power to help us return to His presence one day. This is His work and His glory!"

### HOW DID GOD SHOW UP FOR YOU TODAY?

### WHAT CAN YOU ASK CHRIST TO HELP YOU CARRY RIGHT NOW?

### WHAT IS YOUR HOPE FOR TOMORROW?

DATE    /    /

**Scripture of the Day**

Alma 36:27

"And I have been supported under trials and troubles of every kind, yea, and in all manner of afflictions; yea, God has delivered me from prison, and from bonds, and from death; yea, and I do put my trust in him, and he will still deliver me."

**Quote of the Day**

Brent H. Nielson,
"Is There No Balm in Gilead?"
October 2021

"The Savior's Atonement, which makes available both His redeeming and His enabling power, is the ultimate blessing that Jesus Christ offers to all. As we repent with full purpose of heart, the Savior cleanses us from sin. As we cheerfully submit our will to the Father, even in the most difficult of circumstances, the Savior will lift our burdens and make them light."

### HOW DID GOD SHOW UP FOR YOU TODAY?

### WHAT CAN YOU ASK CHRIST TO HELP YOU CARRY RIGHT NOW?

### WHAT IS YOUR HOPE FOR TOMORROW?

DATE      /      /

**Scripture of the Day**

———

Mosiah 8:18

"God has provided a means that man, through faith, might work mighty miracles; therefore he becometh a great benefit to his fellow beings."

**Quote of the Day**

———

Susan H. Porter, "Lessons at the Well," April 2022

"No matter our circumstances, our lives are sacred and have meaning and purpose. Each of us is a beloved daughter of God, born with divinity in our souls. . . . We can choose to turn to the Savior today for the strength and healing that will enable us to fulfill *all* that we were sent here to do."

### HOW DID GOD SHOW UP FOR YOU TODAY?

### WHAT CAN YOU ASK CHRIST TO HELP YOU CARRY RIGHT NOW?

### WHAT IS YOUR HOPE FOR TOMORROW?

DATE    /    /

## Scripture of the Day

"That which is of God is light; and he that receiveth light, and continueth in God, receiveth more light; and that light groweth brighter and brighter until the perfect day."

*Doctrine and Covenants 50:24*

## Quote of the Day

"As we intensify our faith in Christ, we receive light in intensifying measure until it dispels all darkness that might gather around us. . . . Just as sunlight daily bathes the earth to renew and sustain life, you can daily brighten the light within you when you choose to follow Him—Jesus Christ."

*Timothy J. Dyches, "Light Cleaveth unto Light," April 2021*

### HOW DID GOD SHOW UP FOR YOU TODAY?

### WHAT CAN YOU ASK CHRIST TO HELP YOU CARRY RIGHT NOW?

### WHAT IS YOUR HOPE FOR TOMORROW?

DATE     /     /

**Scripture of the Day**

---

Isaiah 40:31

"But they that wait upon the Lord shall renew their strength; they shall mount up with wings as eagles; they shall run, and not be weary; and they shall walk, and not faint."

**Quote of the Day**

---

Russell M. Nelson, "Make Time for the Lord," October 2021

"The voices and pressures of the world are engaging and numerous. But too many voices are deceptive, seductive, and can pull us off the covenant path. To avoid the inevitable heartbreak that follows, I plead with you today to counter the lure of the world by making time for the Lord in your life—each and every day."

### HOW DID GOD SHOW UP FOR YOU TODAY?

### WHAT CAN YOU ASK CHRIST TO HELP YOU CARRY RIGHT NOW?

### WHAT IS YOUR HOPE FOR TOMORROW?

DATE      /      /

## *Scripture of the Day*

*Luke 11:9–10*

"And I say unto you, Ask, and it shall be given you; seek, and ye shall find; knock, and it shall be opened unto you. For every one that asketh receiveth; and he that seeketh findeth; and to him that knocketh it shall be opened."

## *Quote of the Day*

*Dallin H. Oaks, "The Teachings of Jesus Christ," April 2023*

"We are given the scriptures to direct our lives."

### HOW DID GOD SHOW UP FOR YOU TODAY?

### WHAT CAN YOU ASK CHRIST TO HELP YOU CARRY RIGHT NOW?

### WHAT IS YOUR HOPE FOR TOMORROW?

DATE      /      /

## Scripture of the Day

*2 Corinthians 4:14–15*

"Knowing that he which raised up the Lord Jesus shall raise up us also by Jesus, and shall present us with you. For all things are for your sakes, that the abundant grace might through the thanksgiving of many redound to the glory of God."

## Quote of the Day

*Sharon Eubank, "Turn On Your Light," October 2017*

"Being righteous doesn't mean being perfect or never making mistakes. It means developing an inner connection with God, repenting of our sins and mistakes, and freely helping others."

### HOW DID GOD SHOW UP FOR YOU TODAY?

### WHAT CAN YOU ASK CHRIST TO HELP YOU CARRY RIGHT NOW?

### WHAT IS YOUR HOPE FOR TOMORROW?

DATE    /    /

## Scripture of the Day

*Moroni 7:3–4*

"Wherefore, I would speak unto you that are of the church, that are the peaceable followers of Christ, and that have obtained a sufficient hope by which ye can enter into the rest of the Lord, from this time henceforth until ye shall rest with him in heaven. And now my brethren, I judge these things of you because of your peaceable walk with the children of men."

## Quote of the Day

*D. Todd Christofferson, "One in Christ," April 2023*

"Unity does not require sameness, but it does require harmony. We can have our hearts knit together in love, be one in faith and doctrine, and still cheer for different teams, disagree on various political issues, debate about goals and the right way to achieve them, and many other such things. But we can never disagree or contend with anger or contempt for one another."

#### HOW DID GOD SHOW UP FOR YOU TODAY?

#### WHAT CAN YOU ASK CHRIST TO HELP YOU CARRY RIGHT NOW?

#### WHAT IS YOUR HOPE FOR TOMORROW?

DATE     /     /

## Scripture of the Day
*2 Nephi 28:30*

"For behold, thus saith the Lord God: I will give unto the children of men line upon line, precept upon precept, here a little and there a little; and blessed are those who hearken unto my precepts, and lend an ear unto my counsel, for they shall learn wisdom; for unto him that receiveth I will give more."

## Quote of the Day
*Scott D. Whiting, "Becoming like Him," October 2020*

"You are good enough, you are loved, but that does not mean that you are yet complete. There is work to be done in this life and the next. Only with His divine help can we all progress toward becoming like Him. . . . I know that becoming like Him through His divine help and strength *is* achievable step by step. If not so, He would not have given us this commandment."

### HOW DID GOD SHOW UP FOR YOU TODAY?

### WHAT CAN YOU ASK CHRIST TO HELP YOU CARRY RIGHT NOW?

### WHAT IS YOUR HOPE FOR TOMORROW?

DATE    /    /

## Scripture of the Day

*Doctrine and Covenants 50:44*

"Wherefore, I am in your midst, and I am the good shepherd, and the stone of Israel. He that buildeth upon this rock shall never fall."

## Quote of the Day

*Russell M. Nelson, "The Temple and Your Spiritual Foundation," October 2021*

"When your spiritual foundation is built solidly upon Jesus Christ, you have *no need to fear*. As you are true to your covenants made in the temple, you will be strengthened by His power. Then, when spiritual earthquakes occur, you will be able to stand *strong* because your spiritual foundation is solid and immovable."

### HOW DID GOD SHOW UP FOR YOU TODAY?

### WHAT CAN YOU ASK CHRIST TO HELP YOU CARRY RIGHT NOW?

### WHAT IS YOUR HOPE FOR TOMORROW?

DATE      /      /

## Scripture of the Day

*Exodus 20:7*

"Thou shalt not take the name of the Lord thy God in vain; for the Lord will not hold him guiltless that taketh his name in vain."

## Quote of the Day

*Dale G. Renlund, "Accessing God's Power through Covenants," April 2023*

"To our modern ears, this sounds like a prohibition against irreverently using the Lord's name. The commandment includes that, but its injunction is even more profound. The Hebrew word translated as 'take' means to 'lift up' or 'carry,' as one would a banner that identifies oneself with an individual or group. The word translated as 'vain' means 'empty' or 'deceptive.' The commandment to not take the Lord's name in vain can thus mean, 'You should not identify yourself as a disciple of Jesus Christ unless you intend to represent Him well.'"

### HOW DID GOD SHOW UP FOR YOU TODAY?

### WHAT CAN YOU ASK CHRIST TO HELP YOU CARRY RIGHT NOW?

### WHAT IS YOUR HOPE FOR TOMORROW?

DATE      /      /

## *Scripture of the Day*

"Abide in me, and I in you. . . . If ye abide in me, and my words abide in you, ye shall ask what ye will, and it shall be done unto you."

*John 15:4, 7*

## *Quote of the Day*

"Christ's light brings hope, happiness, and healing of any spiritual wound or ailment. Those who experience this refining influence become instruments in the hands of the Light of the World to give light to others."

*Dieter F. Uchtdorf, "Bearers of Heavenly Light," October 2017*

### HOW DID GOD SHOW UP FOR YOU TODAY?

### WHAT CAN YOU ASK CHRIST TO HELP YOU CARRY RIGHT NOW?

### WHAT IS YOUR HOPE FOR TOMORROW?

DATE      /      /

## Scripture of the Day

*Galatians 6:2*

"Bear ye one another's burdens, and so fulfil the law of Christ."

## Quote of the Day

Russell M. Nelson, "What We Are Learning and Will Never Forget," April 2021

"God wants us to work together and help each other. That is why He sends us to earth in families and organizes us into wards and stakes. That is why He asks us to serve and minister to each other. That is why He asks us to live *in* the world but not be *of* the world. We can accomplish so much more together than we can alone. God's plan of happiness would be frustrated if His children remained isolated one from another."

### HOW DID GOD SHOW UP FOR YOU TODAY?

### WHAT CAN YOU ASK CHRIST TO HELP YOU CARRY RIGHT NOW?

### WHAT IS YOUR HOPE FOR TOMORROW?

DATE      /      /

## *Scripture of the Day*

*Mormon 9:16*

"Behold, are not the things that God hath wrought marvelous in our eyes? Yea, and who can comprehend the marvelous works of God?"

## *Quote of the Day*

*Dallin H. Oaks, "What Has Our Savior Done for Us?" April 2021*

"Our Savior and Redeemer endured incomprehensible suffering to become a sacrifice for the sins of all mortals who would repent. This atoning sacrifice offered the ultimate good, the pure lamb without blemish, for the ultimate measure of evil, the sins of the entire world. It opened the door for each of us to be cleansed of our personal sins so we can be readmitted to the presence of God, our Eternal Father. This open door is available to all of the children of God."

### HOW DID GOD SHOW UP FOR YOU TODAY?

### WHAT CAN YOU ASK CHRIST TO HELP YOU CARRY RIGHT NOW?

### WHAT IS YOUR HOPE FOR TOMORROW?

DATE      /      /

**Scripture of the Day**

*Alma 32:42*

"And because of your diligence and your faith and your patience with the word in nourishing it, that it may take root in you, behold, by and by ye shall pluck the fruit thereof, which is most precious, which is sweet above all that is sweet, and which is white above all that is white, yea, and pure above all that is pure; and ye shall feast upon this fruit even until ye are filled, that ye hunger not, neither shall ye thirst."

**Quote of the Day**

*S. Gifford Nielsen,
"This Is Our Time!"
April 2021*

"Our Heavenly Father wants us to love ourselves—not to become prideful or self-centered, but to see ourselves as He sees us: we are His cherished children. When this truth sinks deep into our hearts, our love for God grows. When we view ourselves with sincere respect, our hearts are open to treat others that way too. The more we recognize our divine worth, the better we understand this divine truth: that God has sent us right here, right now, at this momentous time in history, so that we can do the greatest possible good with the talents and gifts we have."

## HOW DID GOD SHOW UP FOR YOU TODAY?

## WHAT CAN YOU ASK CHRIST TO HELP YOU CARRY RIGHT NOW?

## WHAT IS YOUR HOPE FOR TOMORROW?

DATE        /        /

## Scripture of the Day

*Doctrine and Covenants 18:17–18*

"Behold, you have my gospel before you, and my rock, and my salvation. Ask the Father in my name in faith, believing that you shall receive, and you shall have the Holy Ghost, which manifesteth all things which are expedient unto the children of men."

## Quote of the Day

*Brook P. Hales, "Answers to Prayer," April 2019*

"One aspect of that perfect love is our Heavenly Father's involvement in the details of our lives, even when we may not be aware of it or understand it. We seek the Father's divine guidance and help through heartfelt, earnest prayer. When we honor our covenants and strive to be more like our Savior, we are entitled to a constant stream of divine guidance through the influence and inspiration of the Holy Ghost."

### HOW DID GOD SHOW UP FOR YOU TODAY?

### WHAT CAN YOU ASK CHRIST TO HELP YOU CARRY RIGHT NOW?

### WHAT IS YOUR HOPE FOR TOMORROW?

DATE         /         /

## Scripture of the Day

2 Chronicles 20:17

"Ye shall not need to fight in this battle: set yourselves, stand ye still, and see the salvation of the Lord with you."

## Quote of the Day

Ronald A. Rasband,
"Behold! I Am a
God of Miracles,"
April 2021

"Looking at things through mortal eyes, we want the Lord to intervene, to fix what is broken. Through faith, the miracle will come, though not necessarily on our timetable or with the resolution we desired. Does that mean we are less than faithful or do not merit His intervention? No. We are beloved of the Lord. He gave His life for us, and His Atonement continues to release us from burdens and sin as we repent and draw close to Him."

### HOW DID GOD SHOW UP FOR YOU TODAY?

### WHAT CAN YOU ASK CHRIST TO HELP YOU CARRY RIGHT NOW?

### WHAT IS YOUR HOPE FOR TOMORROW?

DATE      /      /

## *Scripture of the Day*

*John 13:34*

"A new commandment I give unto you, That ye love one another; as I have loved you, that ye also love one another."

## *Quote of the Day*

*Gerrit W. Gong, "Room in the Inn," April 2021*

"As our hearts change and we receive His image in our countenance, we see Him and ourselves in His Church. In Him, we find clarity, not dissonance. In Him, we find cause to do good, reason to be good, and increasing capacity to become better. In Him, we discover abiding faith, liberating selflessness, caring change, and trust in God. In His Inn, we find and deepen our personal relationship with God, our Father, and Jesus Christ."

### HOW DID GOD SHOW UP FOR YOU TODAY?

### WHAT CAN YOU ASK CHRIST TO HELP YOU CARRY RIGHT NOW?

### WHAT IS YOUR HOPE FOR TOMORROW?

DATE    /    /

### *Scripture of the Day*

Matthew 25:6–10

"And at midnight there was a cry made, Behold, the bridegroom cometh; go ye out to meet him. Then all those virgins arose, and trimmed their lamps. And the foolish said unto the wise, Give us of your oil; for our lamps are gone out. But the wise answered, saying, Not so; lest there be not enough for us and you: but go ye rather to them that sell, and buy for yourselves. And while they went to buy, the bridegroom came; and they that were ready went in with him to the marriage: and the door was shut."

### *Quote of the Day*

Ronald A. Rasband, "Hosanna to the Most High God," April 2023

"We, like the ten virgins, have lamps; but do we have oil? . . . Oil comes from believing and acting on prophecy and the words of living prophets. . . . Oil fills our souls when we hear and feel the Holy Ghost and act on that divine guidance. Oil pours into our hearts when our choices show we love the Lord and we love what He loves. Oil comes from repenting and seeking the healing of the Atonement of Jesus Christ."

## HOW DID GOD SHOW UP FOR YOU TODAY?

## WHAT CAN YOU ASK CHRIST TO HELP YOU CARRY RIGHT NOW?

## WHAT IS YOUR HOPE FOR TOMORROW?

DATE      /      /

### *Scripture of the Day*

"And it had come to pass that my father spake unto her, saying: I know that I am a visionary man; for if I had not seen the things of God in a vision I should not have known the goodness of God, but had tarried at Jerusalem, and had perished with my brethren."

1 Nephi 5:4

### *Quote of the Day*

"As you proceed firmly in Christ and with courage not only to proclaim the truth but to live the truth, you will find comfort and peace during the turbulence that you shall encounter in these days."

Denelson Silva,
"Courage to Proclaim the Truth,"
October 2022

## HOW DID GOD SHOW UP FOR YOU TODAY?

## WHAT CAN YOU ASK CHRIST TO HELP YOU CARRY RIGHT NOW?

## WHAT IS YOUR HOPE FOR TOMORROW?

DATE      /      /

### Scripture of the Day

*Mosiah 5:7*

"And now, because of the covenant which ye have made ye shall be called the children of Christ, his sons, and his daughters; for behold, this day he hath spiritually begotten you; for ye say that your hearts are changed through faith on his name; therefore, ye are born of him and have become his sons and his daughters."

### Quote of the Day

Quentin L. Cook, "Safely Gathered Home," April 2023

"Our Heavenly Father's plan for safely gathering His children to our heavenly home is not based on worldly success, economic status, education, race, or gender. Father's plan is based on righteousness, keeping His commandments, and receiving sacred ordinances and honoring the covenants we make."

#### HOW DID GOD SHOW UP FOR YOU TODAY?

#### WHAT CAN YOU ASK CHRIST TO HELP YOU CARRY RIGHT NOW?

#### WHAT IS YOUR HOPE FOR TOMORROW?

DATE    /    /

## *Scripture of the Day*

*Doctrine and Covenants 58:3*

"Ye cannot behold with your natural eyes, for the present time, the design of your God concerning those things which shall come hereafter, and the glory which shall follow after much tribulation."

## *Quote of the Day*

*Henry B. Eyring, "Tested, Proved, and Polished," October 2020*

"The greatest blessing that will come when we prove ourselves faithful to our covenants during our trials will be a change in our natures. By our choosing to keep our covenants, the power of Jesus Christ and the blessings of His Atonement can work in us. Our hearts can be softened to love, to forgive, and to invite others to come unto the Savior. Our confidence in the Lord increases. Our fears decrease."

### HOW DID GOD SHOW UP FOR YOU TODAY?

### WHAT CAN YOU ASK CHRIST TO HELP YOU CARRY RIGHT NOW?

### WHAT IS YOUR HOPE FOR TOMORROW?

DATE    /    /

**Scripture of the Day**

"I have fought a good fight, I have finished my course, I have kept the faith."

*2 Timothy 4:7*

**Quote of the Day**

"Minutes and hours well spent are the building blocks of a life well lived. They can inspire goodness, lift us from the captivity of imperfections, and lead us upward to the redemptive path of forgiveness and sanctification."

*Dieter F. Uchtdorf, "Daily Restoration," October 2021*

### HOW DID GOD SHOW UP FOR YOU TODAY?

### WHAT CAN YOU ASK CHRIST TO HELP YOU CARRY RIGHT NOW?

### WHAT IS YOUR HOPE FOR TOMORROW?

DATE      /      /

### *Scripture of the Day*

*Matthew 22:37–39*

"Jesus said unto him, Thou shalt love the Lord thy God with all thy heart, and with all thy soul, and with all thy mind. This is the first and great commandment. And the second is like unto it, Thou shalt love thy neighbour as thyself."

### *Quote of the Day*

*Jeffrey R. Holland, "The Greatest Possession," October 2021*

"We are speaking here of the first great commandment given to the human family—to love God wholeheartedly, without reservation or compromise, that is, with all our heart, might, mind, and strength. This love of God is the first great *commandment* in the universe. But the first great *truth* in the universe is that *God loves us* exactly that way—wholeheartedly, without reservation or compromise, with all of *His* heart, might, mind, and strength. And when those majestic forces from His heart and ours meet without restraint, there is a veritable explosion of spiritual, moral power."

#### HOW DID GOD SHOW UP FOR YOU TODAY?

#### WHAT CAN YOU ASK CHRIST TO HELP YOU CARRY RIGHT NOW?

#### WHAT IS YOUR HOPE FOR TOMORROW?

DATE   /   /

## *Scripture of the Day*

*Luke 8:49–50*

"While he yet spake, there cometh one from the ruler of the synagogue's house, saying to him, Thy daughter is dead; trouble not the Master. But when Jesus heard it, he answered him, saying, Fear not: believe only, and she shall be made whole."

## *Quote of the Day*

*Patrick Kearon, "He Is Risen with Healing in His Wings: We Can Be More Than Conquerors," April 2022*

"Jesus specializes in the seemingly impossible. He came here to make the impossible possible, the irredeemable redeemable, to heal the unhealable, to right the unrightable, to promise the unpromisable. And He's really good at it. In fact, He's perfect at it."

### HOW DID GOD SHOW UP FOR YOU TODAY?

### WHAT CAN YOU ASK CHRIST TO HELP YOU CARRY RIGHT NOW?

### WHAT IS YOUR HOPE FOR TOMORROW?

DATE       /       /

## Scripture of the Day

*2 Nephi 4:19*

"And when I desire to rejoice, my heart groaneth because of my sins; nevertheless, I know in whom I have trusted."

## Quote of the Day

*John A. McCune, "Come unto Christ—Living as Latter-day Saints," April 2020*

"As followers of Christ, we are not spared challenges and trials in our lives. We are often required to do difficult things that, if attempted alone, would be overwhelming and may be impossible. As we accept the Savior's invitation to 'come unto me,' He will provide the support, comfort, and peace that are necessary, just as He did for Nephi and Joseph. Even in our deepest trials, we can feel the warm embrace of His love as we trust Him and accept His will."

### HOW DID GOD SHOW UP FOR YOU TODAY?

### WHAT CAN YOU ASK CHRIST TO HELP YOU CARRY RIGHT NOW?

### WHAT IS YOUR HOPE FOR TOMORROW?

DATE     /     /

## Scripture of the Day

*3 Nephi 17:7*

"Have ye any that are sick among you? Bring them hither. Have ye any that are lame, or blind, or halt, or maimed, or leprous, or that are withered, or that are deaf, or that are afflicted in any manner? Bring them hither and I will heal them, for I have compassion upon you; my bowels are filled with mercy."

## Quote of the Day

*Peter F. Meurs, "He Could Heal Me!" April 2023*

"When our Savior, Jesus Christ, looks upon us, He sees and understands the pain and burden of our sins. He sees our addictions and challenges. He sees our struggles and afflictions of any kind—and He is filled with compassion toward us."

### HOW DID GOD SHOW UP FOR YOU TODAY?

### WHAT CAN YOU ASK CHRIST TO HELP YOU CARRY RIGHT NOW?

### WHAT IS YOUR HOPE FOR TOMORROW?

DATE        /        /

## Scripture of the Day

*1 Samuel 16:7*

"The Lord seeth not as man seeth; for man looketh on the outward appearance, but the Lord looketh on the heart."

## Quote of the Day

*Michelle D. Craig, "Eyes to See," October 2020*

"I witness that Jesus Christ loves us and can give us eyes to see—*even* when it's hard, *even* when we're tired, *even* when we're lonely, and *even* when the outcomes are not as we hoped. Through His grace, He will bless us and increase our capacity. Through the power of the Holy Ghost, Christ will enable us to *see* ourselves and *see* others as He does. With His help, we can discern what is most needful. We can begin to see the hand of the Lord working in and through the ordinary details of our lives—we will see deeply."

### HOW DID GOD SHOW UP FOR YOU TODAY?

### WHAT CAN YOU ASK CHRIST TO HELP YOU CARRY RIGHT NOW?

### WHAT IS YOUR HOPE FOR TOMORROW?

DATE  /  /

## *Scripture of the Day*

*Psalm 91:11*

"For he shall give his angels charge over thee, to keep thee in all thy ways."

## *Quote of the Day*

*Gerrit W. Gong,
"Ministering,"
April 2023*

"Jesus Christ ministers. Angels minister. . . . As we minister as He would, we witness His miracles, His blessings."

### HOW DID GOD SHOW UP FOR YOU TODAY?

### WHAT CAN YOU ASK CHRIST TO HELP YOU CARRY RIGHT NOW?

### WHAT IS YOUR HOPE FOR TOMORROW?

DATE        /        /

## Scripture of the Day

*Acts 4:32*

"And the multitude of them that believed were of one heart and of one soul: neither said any of them that ought of the things which he possessed was his own; but they had all things common."

## Quote of the Day

L. Todd Budge, "Giving Holiness to the Lord," October 2021

"In modern usage, the term *sacrifice* has come to connote the concept of 'giving up' things for the Lord and His kingdom. However, in ancient days, the meaning of the word *sacrifice* was more closely tied to its two Latin roots: *sacer*, meaning 'sacred' or 'holy,' and *facere*, meaning 'to make.' Thus, anciently *sacrifice* meant literally 'to make something or someone holy.' Viewed as such, sacrifice is a process of becoming holy and coming to know God, not an event or ritualistic 'giving up' of things for the Lord."

### HOW DID GOD SHOW UP FOR YOU TODAY?

### WHAT CAN YOU ASK CHRIST TO HELP YOU CARRY RIGHT NOW?

### WHAT IS YOUR HOPE FOR TOMORROW?

DATE      /      /

## *Scripture of the Day*

*Luke 12:27–28*

"Consider the lilies how they grow: they toil not, they spin not; and yet I say unto you, that Solomon in all his glory was not arrayed like one of these. If then God so clothe the grass, which is to day in the field, and to morrow is cast into the oven; how much more will he clothe you, O ye of little faith?"

## *Quote of the Day*

*Neil L. Andersen, "My Mind Caught Hold upon This Thought of Jesus Christ," April 2023*

"You have lived with your own individual identity long before coming to earth."

### HOW DID GOD SHOW UP FOR YOU TODAY?

### WHAT CAN YOU ASK CHRIST TO HELP YOU CARRY RIGHT NOW?

### WHAT IS YOUR HOPE FOR TOMORROW?

DATE      /      /

## Scripture of the Day

"Ye are free; ye are permitted to act for yourselves; for behold, God hath given unto you a knowledge and he hath made you free."

*Helaman 14:30*

## Quote of the Day

"God intends that His children should act according to the moral agency He has given them, 'that every man may be accountable for his own sins in the day of judgment.' It is His plan and His will that we have the principal decision-making role in our own life's drama."

*D. Todd Christofferson, "Free Forever, to Act for Themselves," October 2014*

### HOW DID GOD SHOW UP FOR YOU TODAY?

### WHAT CAN YOU ASK CHRIST TO HELP YOU CARRY RIGHT NOW?

### WHAT IS YOUR HOPE FOR TOMORROW?

DATE        /         /

## Scripture of the Day

*Alma 36:20*

"And oh, what joy, and what marvelous light I did behold; yea, my soul was filled with joy as exceeding as was my pain!"

## Quote of the Day

*Neal A. Maxwell, "Endure It Well," April 1990*

"By taking Jesus' yoke upon us and enduring, we learn most deeply of Him and especially how to be like Him. . . . Moreover, we find that sorrow can actually enlarge the mind and heart in order to 'give place,' expanded space for later joy."

### HOW DID GOD SHOW UP FOR YOU TODAY?

### WHAT CAN YOU ASK CHRIST TO HELP YOU CARRY RIGHT NOW?

### WHAT IS YOUR HOPE FOR TOMORROW?

DATE      /      /

### Scripture of the Day

*Doctrine and Covenants 20:37*

"All those who humble themselves before God, and desire to be baptized, and come forth with broken hearts and contrite spirits, and witness before the church that they have truly repented of all their sins, and are willing to take upon them the name of Jesus Christ, having a determination to serve him to the end, and truly manifest by their works that they have received of the Spirit of Christ unto the remission of their sins, shall be received by baptism into his church."

### Quote of the Day

*Quentin L. Cook, "Safely Gathered Home," April 2023*

"Please understand that there are remarkable blessings in sharing the gospel of Jesus Christ. The scriptures speak of joy and peace, forgiveness of sins, protection from temptations, and sustaining power from God."

#### HOW DID GOD SHOW UP FOR YOU TODAY?

#### WHAT CAN YOU ASK CHRIST TO HELP YOU CARRY RIGHT NOW?

#### WHAT IS YOUR HOPE FOR TOMORROW?

DATE      /      /

## Scripture of the Day

*Exodus 14:21–22*

"And Moses stretched out his hand over the sea; and the Lord caused the sea to go back by a strong east wind all that night, and made the sea dry land, and the waters were divided. And the children of Israel went into the midst of the sea upon the dry ground: and the waters were a wall unto them on their right hand, and on their left."

## Quote of the Day

*Gordon B. Hinckley, "If Ye Be Willing and Obedient," October 1971*

"God will always make a way where there is no way."

### HOW DID GOD SHOW UP FOR YOU TODAY?

### WHAT CAN YOU ASK CHRIST TO HELP YOU CARRY RIGHT NOW?

### WHAT IS YOUR HOPE FOR TOMORROW?

DATE    /    /

## Scripture of the Day

"But let patience have her perfect work, that ye may be perfect and entire, wanting nothing."

*James 1:4*

## Quote of the Day

"In our efforts to find joy in the midst of our trials, we had forgotten that having patience is the key to letting those trials work for our good. . . . Just as the trying of our faith works patience within us, when we exercise patience, our faith increases. As our faith increases, so does our joy."

*Jeremy R. Jaggi, "Let Patience Have Her Perfect Work, and Count It All Joy!" October 2020*

### HOW DID GOD SHOW UP FOR YOU TODAY?

### WHAT CAN YOU ASK CHRIST TO HELP YOU CARRY RIGHT NOW?

### WHAT IS YOUR HOPE FOR TOMORROW?

DATE    /    /

### Scripture of the Day

*Matthew 6:19–21, 33*

"Lay not up for yourselves treasures upon earth, where moth and rust doth corrupt, and where thieves break through and steal: But lay up for yourselves treasures in heaven, where neither moth nor rust doth corrupt, and where thieves do not break through nor steal: For where your treasure is, there will your heart be also. . . . But seek ye first the kingdom of God, and his righteousness; and all these things shall be added unto you."

### Quote of the Day

*Michael A. Dunn, "One Percent Better," October 2021*

"I invite you to examine your life and see what's stagnated or slowed you on the covenant pathway. Then look broader. Seek modest but makeable fixes in your life that might result in the sweet joy of being just a little better."

#### HOW DID GOD SHOW UP FOR YOU TODAY?

#### WHAT CAN YOU ASK CHRIST TO HELP YOU CARRY RIGHT NOW?

#### WHAT IS YOUR HOPE FOR TOMORROW?

DATE        /        /

## Scripture of the Day

"And by the power of the Holy Ghost ye may know the truth of all things."

*Moroni 10:5*

## Quote of the Day

"Reflecting on God's goodness and mercy helps us become more spiritually receptive. In turn, increased spiritual sensitivity allows us to come to know the truth of all things by the power of the Holy Ghost."

*Dale G. Renlund, "Consider the Goodness and Greatness of God," April 2020*

### HOW DID GOD SHOW UP FOR YOU TODAY?

### WHAT CAN YOU ASK CHRIST TO HELP YOU CARRY RIGHT NOW?

### WHAT IS YOUR HOPE FOR TOMORROW?

DATE    /    /

## Scripture of the Day

*Alma 8:16, 18*

"And behold, I am sent to command thee that thou return to the city of Ammonihah, and preach again unto the people of the city; yea, preach unto them. Yea, say unto them, except they repent the Lord God will destroy them. . . . Now it came to pass that after Alma had received his message from the angel of the Lord he returned speedily to the land of Ammonihah. And he entered the city by another way, yea, by the way which is on the south of the city of Ammonihah."

## Quote of the Day

*Milton Camargo, "Ask, Seek, and Knock," October 2020*

"What do we learn from Alma about asking, seeking, and knocking? We learn that prayer requires spiritual labor, and it does not always lead to the outcome we hope for. But when we feel discouraged or weighed down with sorrow, the Lord gives us comfort and strength in different ways. He may not answer all of our questions or solve all of our problems right away; rather, He encourages us to keep trying. If we then speedily align our plan with His plan, He will open the way for us, as He did for Alma."

### HOW DID GOD SHOW UP FOR YOU TODAY?

### WHAT CAN YOU ASK CHRIST TO HELP YOU CARRY RIGHT NOW?

### WHAT IS YOUR HOPE FOR TOMORROW?

DATE      /      /

## Scripture of the Day

*Doctrine and Covenants 64:33–34*

"Wherefore, be not weary in well-doing, for ye are laying the foundation of a great work. And out of small things proceedeth that which is great. Behold, the Lord requireth the heart and a willing mind; and the willing and obedient shall eat the good of the land of Zion in these last days."

## Quote of the Day

*Neil L. Andersen, "Drawing Closer to the Savior," October 2022*

"As we know very well, having faith in Jesus Christ and being a true disciple is more than a one-time decision—more than a one-time event. It is a sacred, ongoing process that grows and expands through the seasons of our lives, continuing until we kneel at His feet."

### HOW DID GOD SHOW UP FOR YOU TODAY?

### WHAT CAN YOU ASK CHRIST TO HELP YOU CARRY RIGHT NOW?

### WHAT IS YOUR HOPE FOR TOMORROW?

DATE     /     /

## Scripture of the Day

"Be of good courage, and he shall strengthen your heart, all ye that hope in the Lord."

*Psalm 31:24*

## Quote of the Day

"I emphasize the absolute comprehensiveness of the Savior's plea. He yearns to bless with His grace and mercy every single person who now lives, who has ever lived, and who will yet live upon the earth."

*David A. Bednar, "Abide in Me, and I in You; Therefore Walk with Me," April 2023*

### HOW DID GOD SHOW UP FOR YOU TODAY?

### WHAT CAN YOU ASK CHRIST TO HELP YOU CARRY RIGHT NOW?

### WHAT IS YOUR HOPE FOR TOMORROW?

DATE        /        /

## Scripture of the Day

*Romans 8:38–39*

"For I am persuaded, that neither death, nor life, nor angels, nor principalities, nor powers, nor things present, nor things to come, nor height, nor depth, nor any other creature, shall be able to separate us from the love of God, which is in Christ Jesus our Lord."

## Quote of the Day

*Jeffrey R. Holland, "Lifted Up upon the Cross," October 2022*

"It is one of the most powerful paradoxes of the Crucifixion that the arms of the Savior were stretched wide open and then nailed there, unwittingly but accurately portraying that every man, woman, and child in the entire human family is not only welcome but invited into His redeeming, exalting embrace."

### HOW DID GOD SHOW UP FOR YOU TODAY?

### WHAT CAN YOU ASK CHRIST TO HELP YOU CARRY RIGHT NOW?

### WHAT IS YOUR HOPE FOR TOMORROW?

DATE      /      /

### Scripture of the Day

*Mark 4:37–39*

"And there arose a great storm of wind, and the waves beat into the ship, so that it was now full. And he was in the hinder part of the ship, asleep on a pillow: and they awake him, and say unto him, Master, carest thou not that we perish? And he arose, and rebuked the wind, and said unto the sea, Peace, be still. And the wind ceased, and there was a great calm."

### Quote of the Day

*Mark A. Bragg, "Christlike Poise," April 2023*

"It is through Christ and His Atonement that all good things come into our lives. As we remember who we are, knowing that there is a divine plan of mercy and drawing courage in the strength of the Lord, we can do all things. We will find calm. We will be good women and men in any storm."

#### HOW DID GOD SHOW UP FOR YOU TODAY?

#### WHAT CAN YOU ASK CHRIST TO HELP YOU CARRY RIGHT NOW?

#### WHAT IS YOUR HOPE FOR TOMORROW?

DATE    /    /

## *Scripture of the Day*

2 Nephi 5:27

"And it came to pass that we lived after the manner of happiness."

## *Quote of the Day*

Jonathan S. Schmitt,
"That They Might Know Thee,"
October 2022

"Today, as our world is frequently polarized and divided, there is a great need for us to preach and practice positivity, optimism, and hope. Despite any challenges in our past, faith always points toward the future, filled with hope, allowing us to fulfill Jesus's invitation to be of good cheer. Joyfully living the gospel helps us to become *disciples of good things to come*."

### HOW DID GOD SHOW UP FOR YOU TODAY?

### WHAT CAN YOU ASK CHRIST TO HELP YOU CARRY RIGHT NOW?

### WHAT IS YOUR HOPE FOR TOMORROW?

DATE     /     /

## Scripture of the Day

*1 Nephi 4:1*

"And it came to pass that I spake unto my brethren, saying: Let us go up again unto Jerusalem, and let us be faithful in keeping the commandments of the Lord; for behold he is mightier than all the earth, then why not mightier than Laban and his fifty, yea, or even than his tens of thousands?"

## Quote of the Day

*Matthew S. Holland, "The Exquisite Gift of the Son," October 2020*

"For anyone today with pains so intense or so unique that you feel no one else could fully appreciate them, you may have a point. There may be no family member, friend, or priesthood leader—however sensitive and well-meaning each may be—who knows exactly what you are feeling or has the precise words to help you heal. But know this: there is One who understands perfectly what you are experiencing, who is 'mightier than all the earth,' and who is 'able to do exceeding abundantly above all that [you] ask or think.' The process will unfold in His way and on His schedule, but Christ stands ready *always* to heal every ounce and aspect of your agony. As you allow Him to do so, you will discover that your suffering was not in vain."

### HOW DID GOD SHOW UP FOR YOU TODAY?

### WHAT CAN YOU ASK CHRIST TO HELP YOU CARRY RIGHT NOW?

### WHAT IS YOUR HOPE FOR TOMORROW?

DATE      /      /

## *Scripture of the Day*

"Verily I say, men should be anxiously engaged in a good cause, and do many things of their own free will, and bring to pass much righteousness."

*Doctrine and Covenants 58:27*

## *Quote of the Day*

"The Lord loves effort, and effort brings rewards. We keep practicing. We are always progressing as long as we are striving to follow the Lord. He doesn't expect perfection today."

*Joy D. Jones, "An Especially Noble Calling," April 2020*

### HOW DID GOD SHOW UP FOR YOU TODAY?

### WHAT CAN YOU ASK CHRIST TO HELP YOU CARRY RIGHT NOW?

### WHAT IS YOUR HOPE FOR TOMORROW?

DATE      /      /

## *Scripture of the Day*

*2 Kings 6:17*

"And Elisha prayed, and said, Lord, I pray thee, open his eyes, that he may see. And the Lord opened the eyes of the young man; and he saw: and, behold, the mountain was full of horses and chariots of fire round about Elisha."

## *Quote of the Day*

*Michelle D. Craig, "Eyes to See," October 2020*

"There may be times when you, like the servant, find yourself struggling to see how God is working in your life—times when *you* feel under siege—when the trials of mortality bring you to your knees. Wait and trust in God and in His timing, because you can trust His heart with all of yours. My dear sisters and brothers, you too can pray for the Lord to open your eyes to see things you would not normally see."

### HOW DID GOD SHOW UP FOR YOU TODAY?

### WHAT CAN YOU ASK CHRIST TO HELP YOU CARRY RIGHT NOW?

### WHAT IS YOUR HOPE FOR TOMORROW?

DATE      /      /

## Scripture of the Day

*Matthew 10:29–31*

"Are not two sparrows sold for a farthing? and one of them shall not fall on the ground without your Father. But the very hairs of your head are all numbered. Fear ye not therefore, ye are of more value than many sparrows."

## Quote of the Day

*Gerrit W. Gong, "We Each Have a Story," April 2022*

"Whatever the total number of individuals who have lived on the earth, it is finite, countable, one person at a time. You and I, we each matter."

### HOW DID GOD SHOW UP FOR YOU TODAY?

### WHAT CAN YOU ASK CHRIST TO HELP YOU CARRY RIGHT NOW?

### WHAT IS YOUR HOPE FOR TOMORROW?

DATE    /    /

## Scripture of the Day

"If ye love me, keep my commandments."

*John 14:15*

## Quote of the Day

"We need to believe in Jesus and in God's plan of happiness. To *believe* is to love and follow our Savior and keep the commandments, even in the midst of trials and strife."

*M. Russell Ballard,*
*"Lovest Thou Me*
*More Than These?"*
*October 2021*

### HOW DID GOD SHOW UP FOR YOU TODAY?

### WHAT CAN YOU ASK CHRIST TO HELP YOU CARRY RIGHT NOW?

### WHAT IS YOUR HOPE FOR TOMORROW?

DATE    /    /

## Scripture of the Day

"Therefore, cheer up your hearts, and remember that ye are free to act for yourselves—to choose the way of everlasting death or the way of eternal life."

*2 Nephi 10:23*

## Quote of the Day

"We have Jesus Christ's perfect example to follow, and the journey toward our eternal home is possible only because of His teachings, His life, and His atoning sacrifice—including His death and glorious Resurrection."

*José A. Teixeira, "Remember Your Way Back Home," April 2021*

### HOW DID GOD SHOW UP FOR YOU TODAY?

### WHAT CAN YOU ASK CHRIST TO HELP YOU CARRY RIGHT NOW?

### WHAT IS YOUR HOPE FOR TOMORROW?

DATE    /    /

## Scripture of the Day

*3 Nephi 11:39*

"Verily, verily, I say unto you, that this is my doctrine, and whoso buildeth upon this buildeth upon my rock, and the gates of hell shall not prevail against them."

## Quote of the Day

*W. Mark Bassett, "After the Fourth Day," April 2023*

"We know that 'faith [in the Lord Jesus Christ] is a principle of action' and 'miracles do not produce faith, but strong faith is developed by obedience to the gospel of Jesus Christ. In other words, faith comes by righteousness.' As we strive to act righteously by making and keeping sacred covenants and applying the doctrine of Christ in our lives, our faith will not only be sufficient to carry us to the fourth day, but with the Lord's help we will also be capable of moving stones that are in our path, arising from despair, and loosening ourselves of all that binds us. While the Lord expects us to 'do all things that lie in our power,' remember that He will provide needed help in all these things as we trust in Him."

### HOW DID GOD SHOW UP FOR YOU TODAY?

### WHAT CAN YOU ASK CHRIST TO HELP YOU CARRY RIGHT NOW?

### WHAT IS YOUR HOPE FOR TOMORROW?

DATE      /      /

**Scripture of the Day**

*Doctrine and Covenants 100:5–6*

"Therefore, verily I say unto you, lift up your voices unto this people; speak the thoughts that I shall put into your hearts, and you shall not be confounded before men; for it shall be given you in the very hour, yea, in the very moment, what ye shall say."

**Quote of the Day**

*Carl B. Cook, "Just Keep Going—with Faith," April 2023*

"Regardless of the size, scope, and seriousness of the challenges we face in life, we all have times when we feel like stopping, leaving, escaping, or possibly giving up. But exercising faith in our Savior, Jesus Christ, helps us overcome discouragement no matter what obstacles we encounter. Just as the Savior finished the work He was given to do, He has the power to help us finish the work we have been given."

## HOW DID GOD SHOW UP FOR YOU TODAY?

## WHAT CAN YOU ASK CHRIST TO HELP YOU CARRY RIGHT NOW?

## WHAT IS YOUR HOPE FOR TOMORROW?

DATE ___/___/___

## Scripture of the Day

*Deuteronomy 6:5*

"And thou shalt love the Lord thy God with all thine heart, and with all thy soul, and with all thy might."

## Quote of the Day

*Henry B. Eyring, "Finding Personal Peace," April 2023*

"Some of you, perhaps many, are not feeling the peace the Lord promised. You may have prayed for personal peace and spiritual comfort. Yet you may feel that the heavens are silent to your pleading for peace. There is an enemy of your soul who does not want you and those you love to find peace. . . . Yet there is reason for optimism: it is that the Light of Christ is placed in every newborn child. With that universal gift comes a sense of what is right, a desire to love and be loved."

### HOW DID GOD SHOW UP FOR YOU TODAY?

### WHAT CAN YOU ASK CHRIST TO HELP YOU CARRY RIGHT NOW?

### WHAT IS YOUR HOPE FOR TOMORROW?

DATE    /    /

**Scripture of the Day**

―――

Hebrews 2:10

"For it became him, for whom are all things, and by whom are all things, in bringing many sons unto glory, to make the captain of their salvation perfect through sufferings."

**Quote of the Day**

―――

Matthew S. Holland, "The Exquisite Gift of the Son," October 2020

"You see, the very nature of God and aim of our earthly existence is happiness, but we cannot become perfect beings of divine joy without experiences that test us, sometimes to our very core. Paul says even the Savior Himself was made eternally 'perfect [or complete] through sufferings.' So guard against the satanic whispering that if you were a better person, you would avoid such trials."

### HOW DID GOD SHOW UP FOR YOU TODAY?

### WHAT CAN YOU ASK CHRIST TO HELP YOU CARRY RIGHT NOW?

### WHAT IS YOUR HOPE FOR TOMORROW?

DATE       /       /

## Scripture of the Day

1 Corinthians 2:14

"But the natural man receiveth not the things of the Spirit of God: for they are foolishness unto him: neither can he know them, because they are spiritually discerned."

## Quote of the Day

Scott D. Whiting, "Becoming like Him," October 2020

"The first step on this path to becoming like Jesus Christ is to have the desire to do so. Understanding the admonition to be like Him is good, but that understanding needs to be coupled with a yearning to transform ourselves, one step at a time, beyond the natural man. To develop the desire, we must know who Jesus Christ is. We must know something of His character, and we must look for His attributes in scripture, worship services, and other holy places. As we begin to know more of Him, we will see His attributes reflected in others. This will encourage us on our own quest, for if others can attain in some measure His attributes, so can we."

#### HOW DID GOD SHOW UP FOR YOU TODAY?

#### WHAT CAN YOU ASK CHRIST TO HELP YOU CARRY RIGHT NOW?

#### WHAT IS YOUR HOPE FOR TOMORROW?

DATE      /      /

## Scripture of the Day

*Mormon 9:18–19*

"And who shall say that Jesus Christ did not do many mighty miracles? And there were many mighty miracles wrought by the hands of the apostles. And if there were miracles wrought then, why has God ceased to be a God of miracles and yet be an unchangeable Being? And behold, I say unto you he changeth not; if so he would cease to be God; and he ceaseth not to be God, and is a God of miracles."

## Quote of the Day

*Dieter F. Uchtdorf, "God among Us," April 2021*

"The Savior always teaches timeless truths. They apply to people of every age and in any circumstance. His message was and is a message of hope and belonging—a testimony that God our Heavenly Father has not abandoned His children. That God is among us!"

### HOW DID GOD SHOW UP FOR YOU TODAY?

### WHAT CAN YOU ASK CHRIST TO HELP YOU CARRY RIGHT NOW?

### WHAT IS YOUR HOPE FOR TOMORROW?

DATE    /    /

## Scripture of the Day

*Ether 12:27*

"And if men come unto me I will show unto them their weakness. I give unto men weakness that they may be humble; and my grace is sufficient for all men that humble themselves before me; for if they humble themselves before me, and have faith in me, then will I make weak things become strong unto them."

## Quote of the Day

*Russell M. Nelson, "We Can Do Better and Be Better," April 2019*

"Nothing is more liberating, more ennobling, or more crucial to our individual progression than is a regular, daily focus on repentance. Repentance is not an event; it is a process. It is the key to happiness and peace of mind. When coupled with faith, repentance opens our access to the power of the Atonement of Jesus Christ."

### HOW DID GOD SHOW UP FOR YOU TODAY?

### WHAT CAN YOU ASK CHRIST TO HELP YOU CARRY RIGHT NOW?

### WHAT IS YOUR HOPE FOR TOMORROW?

DATE       /       /

## Scripture of the Day

*Doctrine and Covenants 18:36*

"Wherefore, you can testify that you have heard my voice, and know my words."

## Quote of the Day

*Neil L. Andersen, "Spiritually Defining Memories," April 2020*

"When personal difficulty, doubt, or discouragement darken our path, or when world conditions beyond our control lead us to wonder about the future, the spiritually defining memories from our book of life are like luminous stones that help brighten the road ahead, assuring us that God knows us, loves us, and has sent His Son, Jesus Christ, to help us return home."

### HOW DID GOD SHOW UP FOR YOU TODAY?

### WHAT CAN YOU ASK CHRIST TO HELP YOU CARRY RIGHT NOW?

### WHAT IS YOUR HOPE FOR TOMORROW?

DATE      /      /

## Scripture of the Day

2 Chronicles 32:8

"With us is the Lord our God to help us, and to fight our battles."

## Quote of the Day

Russell M. Nelson, "Christ Is Risen; Faith in Him Will Move Mountains," April 2021

"The Lord understands our mortal weakness. We all falter at times. But He also knows of our great potential. The mustard seed starts small but grows into a tree large enough for birds to nest in its branches. The mustard seed represents a small but *growing* faith. The Lord does not require *perfect* faith for us to have access to His *perfect* power. But He does ask us to believe."

### HOW DID GOD SHOW UP FOR YOU TODAY?

### WHAT CAN YOU ASK CHRIST TO HELP YOU CARRY RIGHT NOW?

### WHAT IS YOUR HOPE FOR TOMORROW?

DATE     /     /

## Scripture of the Day

"And he said unto them, When ye pray, say, Our Father which art in heaven, Hallowed be thy name. Thy kingdom come. Thy will be done, as in heaven, so in earth."

*Luke 11:2*

## Quote of the Day

*Lisa L. Harkness, "Peace, Be Still," October 2020*

"Even in turbulent times, faith in the Lord Jesus Christ is gritty and resilient. It helps us sift through unimportant distractions. It encourages us to keep moving along the covenant path. Faith pushes through discouragement and allows us to face the future with resolve and squared shoulders. It prompts us to ask for rescue and relief as we pray to the Father in the name of His Son. And when prayerful pleas seem to go unanswered, our persistent faith in Jesus Christ produces patience, humility, and the ability to reverently utter the words 'Thy will be done.'"

### HOW DID GOD SHOW UP FOR YOU TODAY?

### WHAT CAN YOU ASK CHRIST TO HELP YOU CARRY RIGHT NOW?

### WHAT IS YOUR HOPE FOR TOMORROW?

DATE     /     /

## *Scripture of the Day*

*2 Timothy 1:7*

"For God hath not given us the spirit of fear; but of power, and of love, and of a sound mind."

## *Quote of the Day*

*S. Gifford Nielsen, "This Is Our Time!" April 2021*

"When we hear stories of God's mighty servants who came before us—like Moses, Mary, Moroni, Alma, Esther, Joseph, and many others—they seem bigger than life. But they were not that different from us. They were regular people who faced challenges. They trusted the Lord. They made the right choices at pivotal moments. And, with faith in Jesus Christ, they performed the works required in their time."

### HOW DID GOD SHOW UP FOR YOU TODAY?

### WHAT CAN YOU ASK CHRIST TO HELP YOU CARRY RIGHT NOW?

### WHAT IS YOUR HOPE FOR TOMORROW?

DATE      /      /

## Scripture of the Day

"Lift up your heads, and rejoice, and put your trust in God . . . that God who brought the children of Israel out of the land of Egypt, and caused that they should walk through the Red Sea on dry ground."

*Mosiah 7:19*

## Quote of the Day

"Yes, we might sometimes want to run away from where we are, but we certainly should never run away from who we are—children of the living God who loves us, who is always ready to forgive us, and who will never, ever forsake us. You are His most precious possession. You are His child, to whom He has given prophets and promises, spiritual gifts and revelations, miracles and messages, and angels on both sides of the veil."

*Jeffrey R. Holland, "Fear Not: Believe Only!" April 2022*

### HOW DID GOD SHOW UP FOR YOU TODAY?

### WHAT CAN YOU ASK CHRIST TO HELP YOU CARRY RIGHT NOW?

### WHAT IS YOUR HOPE FOR TOMORROW?

DATE    /    /

### Scripture of the Day

*Moroni 4:3*

"O God, the Eternal Father, we ask thee in the name of thy Son, Jesus Christ, to bless and sanctify this bread to the souls of all those who partake of it; that they may eat in remembrance of the body of thy Son, and witness unto thee, O God, the Eternal Father, that they are willing to take upon them the name of thy Son, and always remember him, and keep his commandments which he hath given them, that they may always have his Spirit to be with them."

### Quote of the Day

*Russell M. Nelson, "Embrace the Future with Faith," October 2020*

"Each time we have the faith to be obedient to God's laws—even when popular opinions belittle us—or each time we resist entertainment or ideologies that celebrate covenant-breaking, we are *exercising* our faith, which in turn *increases* our faith. . . . Our ultimate security comes as we yoke ourselves to Heavenly Father and Jesus Christ! Life *without* God is a life filled with fear. Life *with* God is a life filled with peace."

#### HOW DID GOD SHOW UP FOR YOU TODAY?

#### WHAT CAN YOU ASK CHRIST TO HELP YOU CARRY RIGHT NOW?

#### WHAT IS YOUR HOPE FOR TOMORROW?

DATE         /         /

## Scripture of the Day

*Doctrine and Covenants 38:27*

"Behold, this I have given unto you as a parable, and it is even as I am. I say unto you, be one; and if ye are not one ye are not mine."

## Quote of the Day

*Ulisses Soares, "Followers of the Prince of Peace," April 2023*

"One of the most evident signs that we are drawing closer to the Savior and becoming more like Him is the loving, patient, and kind way with which we treat our fellow beings, whatever the circumstances."

### HOW DID GOD SHOW UP FOR YOU TODAY?

### WHAT CAN YOU ASK CHRIST TO HELP YOU CARRY RIGHT NOW?

### WHAT IS YOUR HOPE FOR TOMORROW?

DATE   /   /

## Scripture of the Day

*Psalm 118:14*

"The Lord is my strength and song, and is become my salvation."

## Quote of the Day

*Paul V. Johnson, "Be Perfected in Him," October 2022*

"We are children of God with a majestic destiny. . . . When we follow God, He gives us power."

### HOW DID GOD SHOW UP FOR YOU TODAY?

### WHAT CAN YOU ASK CHRIST TO HELP YOU CARRY RIGHT NOW?

### WHAT IS YOUR HOPE FOR TOMORROW?

DATE       /       /

## Scripture of the Day

"Therefore if any man be in Christ, he is a new creature: old things are passed away; behold, all things are become new."

*2 Corinthians 5:17*

## Quote of the Day

"The Lord teaches us individually according to our capacity to learn and how we learn. Our growth is dependent on our willingness, natural curiosity, level of faith, and understanding."

*Vaiangina Sikahema, "A House of Sequential Order," October 2021*

### HOW DID GOD SHOW UP FOR YOU TODAY?

### WHAT CAN YOU ASK CHRIST TO HELP YOU CARRY RIGHT NOW?

### WHAT IS YOUR HOPE FOR TOMORROW?

DATE       /       /

**Scripture of the Day**

───

*Hebrews 11:6*

"But without faith it is impossible to please him: for he that cometh to God must believe that he is, and that he is a rewarder of them that diligently seek him."

**Quote of the Day**

───

*Milton Camargo,
"Ask, Seek,
and Knock,"
October 2020*

"Seeking implies mental and spiritual effort—pondering, testing, trying, and studying. We seek because we trust the Lord's promises. . . . When we seek, we are humbly acknowledging that we still have much to learn, and the Lord will expand our understanding, preparing us to receive more."

## HOW DID GOD SHOW UP FOR YOU TODAY?

## WHAT CAN YOU ASK CHRIST TO HELP YOU CARRY RIGHT NOW?

## WHAT IS YOUR HOPE FOR TOMORROW?

DATE      /      /

## *Scripture of the Day*

*2 Nephi 25:13*

"Behold, they will crucify him; and after he is laid in a sepulchre for the space of three days he shall rise from the dead, with healing in his wings; and all those who shall believe on his name shall be saved in the kingdom of God. Wherefore, my soul delighteth to prophesy concerning him, for I have seen his day, and my heart doth magnify his holy name."

## *Quote of the Day*

*M. Russell Ballard, "Remember What Matters Most," April 2023*

"I invite you to bear your testimony of Jesus Christ more often. Bear testimony of what you know and believe and what you feel, not just of what you are thankful for. Testify of your own experiences of coming to know and love the Savior, of living His teachings, and of His redemptive and enabling power in your life. As you bear testimony of what you know, believe, and feel, the Holy Ghost will confirm the truth to those who earnestly listen to your testimony."

### HOW DID GOD SHOW UP FOR YOU TODAY?

### WHAT CAN YOU ASK CHRIST TO HELP YOU CARRY RIGHT NOW?

### WHAT IS YOUR HOPE FOR TOMORROW?

DATE       /       /

### Scripture of the Day

*Alma 58:11*

"Yea, and it came to pass that the Lord our God did visit us with assurances that he would deliver us; yea, insomuch that he did speak peace to our souls, and did grant unto us great faith, and did cause us that we should hope for our deliverance in him."

### Quote of the Day

*Russell M. Nelson, "Embrace the Future with Faith," October 2020*

"Let us not just *endure* this current season. Let us *embrace the future with faith*! Turbulent times are opportunities for us to thrive spiritually. They are times when our influence can be much more penetrating than in calmer times. I promise that as we create places of security, prepare our minds to be faithful to God, and never stop preparing, God will bless us."

#### HOW DID GOD SHOW UP FOR YOU TODAY?

#### WHAT CAN YOU ASK CHRIST TO HELP YOU CARRY RIGHT NOW?

#### WHAT IS YOUR HOPE FOR TOMORROW?

DATE     /     /

**Scripture of the Day**

"And it shall come to pass that the righteous shall be gathered out from among all nations, and shall come to Zion, singing with songs of everlasting joy."

*Doctrine and Covenants 45:71*

**Quote of the Day**

"Unity is enhanced when people are treated with dignity and respect, even though they are different in outward characteristics."

*Quentin L. Cook, "Hearts Knit in Righteousness and Unity," October 2020*

### HOW DID GOD SHOW UP FOR YOU TODAY?

### WHAT CAN YOU ASK CHRIST TO HELP YOU CARRY RIGHT NOW?

### WHAT IS YOUR HOPE FOR TOMORROW?

DATE     /     /

## Scripture of the Day

*Exodus 14:14*

"The Lord shall fight for you, and ye shall hold your peace."

## Quote of the Day

*Russell M. Nelson, "Christ Is Risen; Faith in Him Will Move Mountains," April 2021*

"Learn about miracles. Miracles come according to your faith in the Lord. Central to that faith is trusting His will and timetable—how and when He will bless you with the miraculous help you desire. Only your unbelief will keep God from blessing you with miracles to move the mountains in your life."

### HOW DID GOD SHOW UP FOR YOU TODAY?

### WHAT CAN YOU ASK CHRIST TO HELP YOU CARRY RIGHT NOW?

### WHAT IS YOUR HOPE FOR TOMORROW?

DATE      /      /

## Scripture of the Day

*Galatians 6:18*

"The grace of our Lord Jesus Christ be with your spirit."

## Quote of the Day

*Anthony D. Perkins, "Remember Thy Suffering Saints, O Lord," October 2021*

"When we keep our sacrament covenant to always remember Him, He promises that His Spirit will be with us. The Spirit gives us strength to endure trials and do what we cannot possibly do on our own. The Spirit can heal us."

### HOW DID GOD SHOW UP FOR YOU TODAY?

### WHAT CAN YOU ASK CHRIST TO HELP YOU CARRY RIGHT NOW?

### WHAT IS YOUR HOPE FOR TOMORROW?

DATE      /      /

## Scripture of the Day

*John 8:12*

"Then spake Jesus again unto them, saying, I am the light of the world: he that followeth me shall not walk in darkness, but shall have the light of life."

## Quote of the Day

*Ulisses Soares, "Jesus Christ: The Caregiver of Our Soul," April 2021*

"Christ is ever aware of the adversities we experience in mortality. He understands all of the bitterness, agony, and physical pain as well as the emotional and spiritual challenges we face. The Savior's bowels are filled with mercy, and He is always ready to succor us. This is possible because He personally experienced and took upon Himself in the flesh the pain of our weakness and infirmities."

### HOW DID GOD SHOW UP FOR YOU TODAY?

### WHAT CAN YOU ASK CHRIST TO HELP YOU CARRY RIGHT NOW?

### WHAT IS YOUR HOPE FOR TOMORROW?

DATE        /        /

### Scripture of the Day

*Helaman 15:7–8*

"As many of them as are brought to the knowledge of the truth, and to know of the wicked and abominable traditions of their fathers, and are led to believe the holy scriptures, yea, the prophecies of the holy prophets, which are written, which leadeth them to faith on the Lord, and unto repentance, which faith and repentance bringeth a change of heart unto them—therefore, as many as have come to this, ye know of yourselves are firm and steadfast in the faith, and in the thing wherewith they have been made free."

### Quote of the Day

*Becky Craven, "Keep the Change," October 2020*

"Enduring to the end means changing to the end. I now understand that I am not starting over with each failed attempt, but that with each try, I am continuing my process of change."

#### HOW DID GOD SHOW UP FOR YOU TODAY?

#### WHAT CAN YOU ASK CHRIST TO HELP YOU CARRY RIGHT NOW?

#### WHAT IS YOUR HOPE FOR TOMORROW?

DATE    /    /

## Scripture of the Day

2 Nephi 4:35

"Yea, I know that God will give liberally to him that asketh. Yea, my God will give me, if I ask not amiss; therefore I will lift up my voice unto thee; yea, I will cry unto thee, my God, the rock of my righteousness. Behold, my voice shall forever ascend up unto thee, my rock and mine everlasting God."

## Quote of the Day

Taniela B. Wakolo, "God Loves His Children," April 2021

"Because of the Savior's sacrifice and ransom, I will no longer refer to my challenges as trials and tribulations but as my learning experiences. . . . [Because] of His perfect and sinless life, I will no longer refer to my shortcomings and lack of abilities as weaknesses but rather as my development opportunities."

### HOW DID GOD SHOW UP FOR YOU TODAY?

### WHAT CAN YOU ASK CHRIST TO HELP YOU CARRY RIGHT NOW?

### WHAT IS YOUR HOPE FOR TOMORROW?

DATE      /      /

## *Scripture of the Day*

*Doctrine and Covenants 58:4–6*

"For after much tribulation come the blessings. Wherefore the day cometh that ye shall be crowned with much glory; the hour is not yet, but is nigh at hand. Remember this, which I tell you before, that you may lay it to heart and receive that which is to follow. Behold, verily I say unto you, for this cause have I sent you—that you might be obedient, and that your hearts might be prepared to bear testimony of the things which are to come."

## *Quote of the Day*

*D. Todd Christofferson, "Our Relationship with God," April 2022*

"God will indeed honor His covenants and promises to each of us. We need not worry about that. The atoning power of Jesus Christ—who descended below all things and then ascended on high and who possesses all power in heaven and in earth—ensures that God can and will fulfill His promises. It is essential that we honor and obey His laws, but not every blessing predicated on obedience to law is shaped, designed, and timed according to our expectations. We do our best but must leave to Him the management of blessings, both temporal and spiritual."

### HOW DID GOD SHOW UP FOR YOU TODAY?

### WHAT CAN YOU ASK CHRIST TO HELP YOU CARRY RIGHT NOW?

### WHAT IS YOUR HOPE FOR TOMORROW?

DATE      /      /

## Scripture of the Day

"Every word of God is pure: he is a shield unto them that put their trust in him."

*Proverbs 30:5*

## Quote of the Day

"We believe in Christ. As members of The Church of Jesus Christ of Latter-day Saints, we worship Him and follow His teachings in the scriptures."

*Dallin H. Oaks, "The Teachings of Jesus Christ," April 2023*

### HOW DID GOD SHOW UP FOR YOU TODAY?

### WHAT CAN YOU ASK CHRIST TO HELP YOU CARRY RIGHT NOW?

### WHAT IS YOUR HOPE FOR TOMORROW?

DATE     /     /

### *Scripture of the Day*

"That the communication of thy faith may become effectual by the acknowledging of every good thing which is in you in Christ Jesus."

*Philemon 1:6*

### *Quote of the Day*

*Dale G. Renlund, "Consider the Goodness and Greatness of God," April 2020*

"By acknowledging that every good thing comes from Jesus Christ, we will communicate our faith more effectively to others. We will have courage when confronted with seemingly impossible tasks and circumstances. We will strengthen our resolve to keep the covenants we have made to follow the Savior. We will be filled with the love of God, want to help those in need without being judgmental, love our children and raise them in righteousness, retain a remission of our sins, and always rejoice. These are the remarkable fruits of remembering God's goodness and mercy."

#### HOW DID GOD SHOW UP FOR YOU TODAY?

#### WHAT CAN YOU ASK CHRIST TO HELP YOU CARRY RIGHT NOW?

#### WHAT IS YOUR HOPE FOR TOMORROW?

DATE        /        /

## Scripture of the Day

*1 John 1:8–9*

"If we say that we have no sin, we deceive ourselves, and the truth is not in us. If we confess our sins, he is faithful and just to forgive us our sins, and to cleanse us from all unrighteousness."

## Quote of the Day

*Ulisses Soares, "In Awe of Christ and His Gospel," April 2022*

"We need to immerse ourselves with faith and real intent in the Savior's teachings, striving to incorporate His attributes into our way of being. In addition, we need to draw nearer to Him through our repentance, seeking His forgiveness and His redeeming power in our lives and keeping His commandments. The Lord Himself promised that He would direct our paths if we would trust in Him with all our hearts, acknowledging Him in all our ways and not leaning on our own understanding."

### HOW DID GOD SHOW UP FOR YOU TODAY?

### WHAT CAN YOU ASK CHRIST TO HELP YOU CARRY RIGHT NOW?

### WHAT IS YOUR HOPE FOR TOMORROW?

DATE     /     /

## Scripture of the Day

*Mosiah 18:9*

"Yea, and are willing to mourn with those that mourn; yea, and comfort those that stand in need of comfort, and to stand as witnesses of God at all times and in all things, and in all places that ye may be in, even until death, that ye may be redeemed of God, and be numbered with those of the first resurrection, that ye may have eternal life."

## Quote of the Day

*Camille N. Johnson, "Jesus Christ Is Relief," April 2023*

"So how does the Savior relieve us of the burdens of living in a fallen world with mortal bodies subject to grief and pain? Often, He performs that kind of relief through us! . . . Our covenantal blessing is to partner with Jesus Christ in providing relief, both temporal and spiritual, to all of God's children. We are a conduit through which He provides relief."

### HOW DID GOD SHOW UP FOR YOU TODAY?

### WHAT CAN YOU ASK CHRIST TO HELP YOU CARRY RIGHT NOW?

### WHAT IS YOUR HOPE FOR TOMORROW?

DATE    /    /

## Scripture of the Day

*Ezekiel 18:31*

"Cast away from you all your transgressions, whereby ye have transgressed; and make you a new heart and a new spirit."

## Quote of the Day

*Russell M. Nelson, "We Can Do Better and Be Better," April 2019*

"Nothing is more liberating, more ennobling, or more crucial to our individual progression than is a regular, daily focus on repentance. Repentance is not an event; it is a process. It is the key to happiness and peace of mind. When coupled with faith, repentance opens our access to the power of the Atonement of Jesus Christ."

### HOW DID GOD SHOW UP FOR YOU TODAY?

### WHAT CAN YOU ASK CHRIST TO HELP YOU CARRY RIGHT NOW?

### WHAT IS YOUR HOPE FOR TOMORROW?

DATE    /    /

## Scripture of the Day

*Doctrine and Covenants 121:1–2*

"O God, where art thou? And where is the pavilion that covereth thy hiding place? How long shall thy hand be stayed, and thine eye, yea thy pure eye, behold from the eternal heavens the wrongs of thy people and of thy servants, and thine ear be penetrated with their cries?"

## Quote of the Day

*Jeffrey R. Holland, "Waiting on the Lord," October 2020*

"So while we work and wait together for the answers to some of our prayers, I offer you my apostolic promise that they are heard and they are answered, though perhaps not at the time or in the way we wanted. But they are *always* answered at the time and in the way an omniscient and eternally compassionate parent should answer them. My beloved brothers and sisters, please understand that He who never sleeps nor slumbers cares for the happiness and ultimate exaltation of His children above all else that a divine being has to do. He is pure love, gloriously personified, and Merciful Father is His name."

### HOW DID GOD SHOW UP FOR YOU TODAY?

### WHAT CAN YOU ASK CHRIST TO HELP YOU CARRY RIGHT NOW?

### WHAT IS YOUR HOPE FOR TOMORROW?

DATE    /    /

## Scripture of the Day

*Joshua 1:9*

"Be strong and of a good courage; be not afraid, neither be thou dismayed: for the Lord thy God is with thee withersoever thou goest."

## Quote of the Day

*David A. Bednar, "But We Heeded Them Not," April 2022*

"Faith focused in and on the Lord Jesus Christ fortifies us with spiritual strength. Faith in the Redeemer is a principle of action and of power. As we act in accordance with the truths of His gospel, we are blessed with the spiritual capacity to press forward through the challenges of mortality while focusing on the joys the Savior offers to us."

### HOW DID GOD SHOW UP FOR YOU TODAY?

### WHAT CAN YOU ASK CHRIST TO HELP YOU CARRY RIGHT NOW?

### WHAT IS YOUR HOPE FOR TOMORROW?

DATE      /      /

## Scripture of the Day

*Luke 5:5–6*

"Master, we have toiled all the night, and have taken nothing: nevertheless at thy word I will let down the net. And when they had this done, they inclosed a great multitude of fishes: and their net brake."

## Quote of the Day

*Denelson Silva, "Courage to Proclaim the Truth," October 2022*

"The knowledge of the truth teaches that when we enter the strait and narrow path that will take us back to the presence of Heavenly Father, there will always be a way to escape these problems; there will always be the possibility of doubting our doubts before doubting our faith; and finally, we have a guarantee that we will never be alone when we go through afflictions, for God visits His people in the midst of their afflictions."

### HOW DID GOD SHOW UP FOR YOU TODAY?

### WHAT CAN YOU ASK CHRIST TO HELP YOU CARRY RIGHT NOW?

### WHAT IS YOUR HOPE FOR TOMORROW?

DATE    /    /

## Scripture of the Day

1 Peter 2:9

"But ye are a chosen generation, a royal priesthood, an holy nation, a peculiar people; that ye should shew forth the praises of him who hath called you out of darkness into his marvellous light."

## Quote of the Day

Ulisses Soares, "Followers of the Prince of Peace," April 2023

"As His followers, we are His peculiar people, called to proclaim His virtues, promoters of the peace so generously offered through Him and His atoning sacrifice. This peace is a gift promised to all who turn their hearts to the Savior and live righteously; such peace gives us the strength to enjoy mortal life and enables us to endure the painful trials of our journey."

### HOW DID GOD SHOW UP FOR YOU TODAY?

### WHAT CAN YOU ASK CHRIST TO HELP YOU CARRY RIGHT NOW?

### WHAT IS YOUR HOPE FOR TOMORROW?

DATE      /      /

**Scripture of the Day**

2 Nephi 8:11

"The redeemed of the Lord shall return, and come with singing unto Zion; and everlasting joy and holiness shall be upon their heads; and they shall obtain gladness and joy; sorrow and mourning shall flee away."

**Quote of the Day**

Anthony D. Perkins, "Remember Thy Suffering Saints, O Our God," October 2021

"Suffering does not mean God is displeased with your life. . . . Whatever the cause of your sufferings, your loving Heavenly Father can direct them to refine your soul. Refined souls can bear others' burdens with true empathy and compassion."

HOW DID GOD SHOW UP FOR YOU TODAY?

WHAT CAN YOU ASK CHRIST TO HELP YOU CARRY RIGHT NOW?

WHAT IS YOUR HOPE FOR TOMORROW?

DATE      /      /

## Scripture of the Day

*Moroni 7:13*

"That which is of God inviteth and enticeth to do good continually. Wherefore, everything which inviteth and enticeth to do good, and to love God, and to serve Him, is inspired of God."

## Quote of the Day

*L. Todd Budge, "Giving Holiness to the Lord," October 2021*

"Freed from the need for love, approval, or appreciation from others, our sacrifices become the purest and deepest expressions of our gratitude and love for the Savior and our fellow men. Any prideful sense of self-sacrifice gives way to feelings of gratitude, generosity, contentment, and joy."

### HOW DID GOD SHOW UP FOR YOU TODAY?

### WHAT CAN YOU ASK CHRIST TO HELP YOU CARRY RIGHT NOW?

### WHAT IS YOUR HOPE FOR TOMORROW?

DATE     /     /

## Scripture of the Day

*Doctrine and Covenants 81:5*

"Wherefore, be faithful; stand in the office which I have appointed unto you; succor the weak, lift up the hands which hang down, and strengthen the feeble knees."

## Quote of the Day

*Camille N. Johnson, "Jesus Christ Is Relief," April 2023*

"What is relief? It is the removal or lightening of something painful, troubling, or burdensome, or the strength to endure it. It refers to a person who takes the place of another. It is the legal correction of a wrong. The Anglo-French word comes from Old French, the word *relever*, or 'to raise up,' and from the Latin *relevare*, or 'raise again.' Brothers and sisters, Jesus Christ is relief."

### HOW DID GOD SHOW UP FOR YOU TODAY?

### WHAT CAN YOU ASK CHRIST TO HELP YOU CARRY RIGHT NOW?

### WHAT IS YOUR HOPE FOR TOMORROW?

DATE        /        /

## *Scripture of the Day*

*Esther 4:14*

"And who knoweth whether thou art come to the kingdom for such a time as this?"

## *Quote of the Day*

*Camille N. Johnson, "Invite Christ to Author Your Story," October 2021*

"Esther's level of courage is rarely asked of us. But letting God prevail, letting Him be the author and finisher of our stories, does require us to keep His commandments and the covenants we have made. It is our commandment and covenant keeping that will open the line of communication for us to receive revelation through the Holy Ghost. And it is through the manifestations of the Spirit that we will feel the Master's hand writing our stories with us."

### HOW DID GOD SHOW UP FOR YOU TODAY?

### WHAT CAN YOU ASK CHRIST TO HELP YOU CARRY RIGHT NOW?

### WHAT IS YOUR HOPE FOR TOMORROW?

DATE    /    /

## Scripture of the Day

*1 Corinthians 12:12–13*

"For as the body is one, and hath many members, and all the members of that one body, being many, are one body: so also is Christ. For by one Spirit are we all baptized into one body, whether we be Jews or Gentiles, whether we be bond or free; and have been all made to drink into one Spirit."

## Quote of the Day

*D. Todd Christofferson, "The Doctrine of Belonging," October 2022*

"The doctrine of belonging comes down to this—each one of us can affirm: Jesus Christ died for me; He thought me worthy of His blood. He loves me and can make all the difference in my life. As I repent, His grace will transform me. I am one with Him in the gospel covenant; I belong in His Church and kingdom; and I belong in His cause to bring redemption to all of God's children."

### HOW DID GOD SHOW UP FOR YOU TODAY?

### WHAT CAN YOU ASK CHRIST TO HELP YOU CARRY RIGHT NOW?

### WHAT IS YOUR HOPE FOR TOMORROW?

DATE    /    /

## Scripture of the Day

"If God be for us, who can be against us?"

*Romans 8:31*

## Quote of the Day

"When the Savior atoned for all mankind, He opened a way that those who follow Him can have access to His healing, strengthening, and redeeming power. These spiritual privileges are available to all who seek to hear Him and follow Him."

*Russell M. Nelson, "The Power of Spiritual Momentum," April 2022*

### HOW DID GOD SHOW UP FOR YOU TODAY?

### WHAT CAN YOU ASK CHRIST TO HELP YOU CARRY RIGHT NOW?

### WHAT IS YOUR HOPE FOR TOMORROW?

DATE    /    /

## Scripture of the Day

*Alma 36:27*

"And I have been supported under trials and troubles of every kind, yea, and in all manner of afflictions; yea, God has delivered me from prison, and from bonds, and from death; yea, and I do put my trust in him, and he will still deliver me."

## Quote of the Day

*Paul V. Johnson, "Be Perfected in Him," October 2022*

"The Savior taught that we 'should be perfect.' This can seem so daunting. I can clearly see my personal inadequacies and am painfully aware of the distance between me and perfection. We may have a tendency to think we have to perfect ourselves, but that is not possible. Following every suggestion in every self-help book in the world will not bring it about. There is only one way and one name whereby perfection comes. We are 'made perfect through Jesus the mediator of the new covenant, who wrought out this perfect atonement through the shedding of his own blood.' Our perfection is only possible through God's grace."

### HOW DID GOD SHOW UP FOR YOU TODAY?

### WHAT CAN YOU ASK CHRIST TO HELP YOU CARRY RIGHT NOW?

### WHAT IS YOUR HOPE FOR TOMORROW?

DATE        /         /

## Scripture of the Day

"All things which are good cometh of God."

*Moroni 7:12*

## Quote of the Day

"When we truly are in awe of Jesus Christ and His gospel, we are happier, we have more enthusiasm for God's work, and we recognize the Lord's hand in all things."

*Ulisses Soares,
"In Awe of Christ
and His Gospel,"
April 2022*

### HOW DID GOD SHOW UP FOR YOU TODAY?

### WHAT CAN YOU ASK CHRIST TO HELP YOU CARRY RIGHT NOW?

### WHAT IS YOUR HOPE FOR TOMORROW?

DATE      /      /

## *Scripture of the Day*

*Doctrine and Covenants 68:6*

"Wherefore, be of good cheer, and do not fear, for I the Lord am with you, and will stand by you; and ye shall bear record of me, even Jesus Christ, that I am the Son of the living God, that I was, that I am, and that I am to come."

## *Quote of the Day*

*Russell M. Nelson, "Make Time for the Lord," October 2021*

"Nothing invites the Spirit more than fixing your focus on Jesus Christ. Talk of Christ, rejoice in Christ, feast upon the words of Christ, and press forward with steadfastness in Christ. Make your Sabbath a delight as you worship Him, partake of the sacrament, and keep His day holy."

### HOW DID GOD SHOW UP FOR YOU TODAY?

### WHAT CAN YOU ASK CHRIST TO HELP YOU CARRY RIGHT NOW?

### WHAT IS YOUR HOPE FOR TOMORROW?

DATE        /        /

### Scripture of the Day

"He shall feed his flock like a shepherd: he shall gather the lambs with his arm, and carry them in his bosom, and shall gently lead those that are with young."

*Isaiah 40:11*

### Quote of the Day

"The gospel of Jesus Christ has the power to unite us. We are ultimately more alike than we are different. As members of God's family, we are truly brothers and sisters."

*M. Russell Ballard,*
*"Hope in Christ,"*
*April 2021*

**HOW DID GOD SHOW UP FOR YOU TODAY?**

**WHAT CAN YOU ASK CHRIST TO HELP YOU CARRY RIGHT NOW?**

**WHAT IS YOUR HOPE FOR TOMORROW?**

DATE    /    /

## Scripture of the Day

*James 1:2–3*

"Count it all joy when ye fall into divers temptations; knowing this, that the trying of your faith worketh patience."

## Quote of the Day

*Dale G. Renlund, "Infuriating Unfairness," April 2021*

"Do not let unfairness harden you or corrode your faith in God. Instead, ask God for help. Increase your appreciation for and reliance on the Savior. Rather than becoming bitter, let Him help you become better."

### HOW DID GOD SHOW UP FOR YOU TODAY?

### WHAT CAN YOU ASK CHRIST TO HELP YOU CARRY RIGHT NOW?

### WHAT IS YOUR HOPE FOR TOMORROW?

DATE    /    /

## Scripture of the Day

*John 11:25–26*

"Jesus said unto her, I am the resurrection, and the life: he that believeth in me, though he were dead, yet shall he live: And whosoever liveth and believeth in me shall never die. Believest thou this?"

## Quote of the Day

*Ronald A. Rasband, "Hosanna to the Most High God," April 2023*

"What began with the heralding of Jesus as the promised Messiah in His triumphant entry into Jerusalem closed with His Crucifixion and Resurrection. By divine design, His atoning sacrifice concluded His mortal ministry, making it possible for us to live with our Heavenly Father for eternity."

### HOW DID GOD SHOW UP FOR YOU TODAY?

### WHAT CAN YOU ASK CHRIST TO HELP YOU CARRY RIGHT NOW?

### WHAT IS YOUR HOPE FOR TOMORROW?

DATE    /    /

## Scripture of the Day

*Mosiah 2:41*

"Consider on the blessed and happy state of those that keep the commandments of God. For behold, they are blessed in all things, both temporal and spiritual; and if they hold out faithful to the end they are received into heaven, that thereby they may dwell with God in a state of never-ending happiness."

## Quote of the Day

*Coleen K. Menlove, "Living Happily Ever After," April 2000*

"The story of our search for happiness is written in such a way that if we continue to trust in God and follow His commandments through the challenging times, even those times will bring us closer to the happiness we are seeking."

### HOW DID GOD SHOW UP FOR YOU TODAY?

### WHAT CAN YOU ASK CHRIST TO HELP YOU CARRY RIGHT NOW?

### WHAT IS YOUR HOPE FOR TOMORROW?

DATE    /    /

## Scripture of the Day

*Alma 36:21*

"Yea, I say unto you, my son, that there could be nothing so exquisite and so bitter as were my pains. Yea, and again I say unto you, my son, that on the other hand, there can be nothing so exquisite and sweet as was my joy."

## Quote of the Day

*Neil L. Andersen, "My Mind Caught Hold upon This Thought of Jesus Christ," April 2023*

"My prayer . . . is that we will more consciously shape, strengthen, and secure this preeminent thought of Jesus Christ in the chambers of our soul, allowing it to eagerly flow into our mind, guide us in what we think and do, and continually bring the sweet joy of the Savior's love."

### HOW DID GOD SHOW UP FOR YOU TODAY?

### WHAT CAN YOU ASK CHRIST TO HELP YOU CARRY RIGHT NOW?

### WHAT IS YOUR HOPE FOR TOMORROW?

DATE      /      /

## Scripture of the Day

*Doctrine and Covenants 38:30*

"I tell you these things because of your prayers; wherefore, treasure up wisdom in your bosoms, lest the wickedness of men reveal these things unto you by their wickedness, in a manner which shall speak in your ears with a voice louder than that which shall shake the earth; but if ye are prepared ye shall not fear."

## Quote of the Day

*Russell M. Nelson, "Opening Message," April 2020*

"Our ultimate quest in life is to prepare to meet our Maker. We do this by striving daily to become more like our Savior, Jesus Christ. And we do *that* as we repent daily and receive His cleansing, healing, and strengthening power. Then we can feel enduring peace and joy, even during turbulent times."

### HOW DID GOD SHOW UP FOR YOU TODAY?

### WHAT CAN YOU ASK CHRIST TO HELP YOU CARRY RIGHT NOW?

### WHAT IS YOUR HOPE FOR TOMORROW?

DATE     /     /

## *Scripture of the Day*

*Isaiah 41:10*

"Fear thou not; for I am with thee: be not dismayed; for I am thy God: I will strengthen thee; yea, I will help thee; yea, I will uphold thee with the right hand of my righteousness."

## *Quote of the Day*

*Dieter F. Uchtdorf, "Jesus Christ Is the Strength of Youth," October 2022*

"I believe the Savior Jesus Christ would want you to see, feel, and know that He is your strength. That with His help, there are no limits to what you can accomplish. That your potential is limitless. He would want you to see yourself the way He sees you."

### HOW DID GOD SHOW UP FOR YOU TODAY?

### WHAT CAN YOU ASK CHRIST TO HELP YOU CARRY RIGHT NOW?

### WHAT IS YOUR HOPE FOR TOMORROW?

DATE      /      /

**Scripture of the Day**

*John 17:21–23*

"That they all may be one; as thou, Father, art in me, and I in thee, that they also may be one in us: that the world may believe that thou hast sent me. And the glory which thou gavest me I have given them; that they may be one, even as we are one: I in them, and thou in me, that they may be made perfect in one; and that the world may know that thou hast sent me, and hast loved them, as thou hast loved me."

**Quote of the Day**

*D. Todd Christofferson, "The Doctrine of Belonging," October 2022*

"We don't join the Church for fellowship alone, important as that is. We join for redemption through the love and grace of Jesus Christ. We join to secure the ordinances of salvation and exaltation for ourselves and those we love on both sides of the veil. We join to participate in a great project to establish Zion in preparation for the Lord's return."

## HOW DID GOD SHOW UP FOR YOU TODAY?

## WHAT CAN YOU ASK CHRIST TO HELP YOU CARRY RIGHT NOW?

## WHAT IS YOUR HOPE FOR TOMORROW?

DATE     /     /

## Scripture of the Day

*Matthew 5:9*

"Blessed are the peacemakers: for they shall be called the children of God."

## Quote of the Day

*Russell M. Nelson, "Peacemakers Needed," April 2023*

"Contention drives away the Spirit—every time. Contention reinforces the false notion that confrontation is the way to resolve differences; but it never is. Contention is a choice. Peacemaking is a choice. You have your agency to choose contention or reconciliation. I urge you to *choose* to be a peacemaker, now and always."

### HOW DID GOD SHOW UP FOR YOU TODAY?

### WHAT CAN YOU ASK CHRIST TO HELP YOU CARRY RIGHT NOW?

### WHAT IS YOUR HOPE FOR TOMORROW?

DATE    /    /

## *Scripture of the Day*

*2 Nephi 26:33*

"For none of these iniquities come of the Lord; for he doeth that which is good among the children of men; and he doeth nothing save it be plain unto the children of men; and he inviteth them all to come unto him and partake of his goodness; and he denieth none that come unto him, black and white, bond and free, male and female; and he remembereth the heathen; and all are alike unto God, both Jew and Gentile."

## *Quote of the Day*

*Dale G. Renlund, "The Peace of Christ Abolishes Enmity," October 2021*

"Unity requires effort. It develops when we cultivate the love of God in our hearts and we focus on our eternal destiny. We are united by our common, primary identity as children of God and our commitment to the truths of the restored gospel. In turn, our love of God and our discipleship of Jesus Christ generate genuine concern for others. We value the kaleidoscope of others' characteristics, perspectives, and talents."

### HOW DID GOD SHOW UP FOR YOU TODAY?

### WHAT CAN YOU ASK CHRIST TO HELP YOU CARRY RIGHT NOW?

### WHAT IS YOUR HOPE FOR TOMORROW?

DATE      /      /

**Scripture of the Day**

"I will not boast of myself, but I will boast of my God, for in his strength I can do all things."

*Alma 26:12*

**Quote of the Day**

"Regardless of how insignificant our efforts may seem, if we are sincere, the Savior will use us to accomplish His work. If we simply do the best we can and trust Him to make up the difference, we can become part of the miracles that surround us."

*Vern P. Stanfill, "The Imperfect Harvest," April 2023*

### HOW DID GOD SHOW UP FOR YOU TODAY?

### WHAT CAN YOU ASK CHRIST TO HELP YOU CARRY RIGHT NOW?

### WHAT IS YOUR HOPE FOR TOMORROW?

DATE    /    /

## *Scripture of the Day*

*Jacob 4:10*

"Seek not to counsel the Lord, but to take counsel from his hand. For behold, ye yourselves know that he counseleth in wisdom, and in justice, and in great mercy, over all his works."

## *Quote of the Day*

*José A. Teixeira, "Remember Your Way Back Home," April 2021*

"Make time regularly to boost your spiritual immune system by remembering the blessings you have received from the Lord. Trust the guides you have been given from Him, rather than turning solely to the world to measure your personal worth and find your way."

### HOW DID GOD SHOW UP FOR YOU TODAY?

### WHAT CAN YOU ASK CHRIST TO HELP YOU CARRY RIGHT NOW?

### WHAT IS YOUR HOPE FOR TOMORROW?

DATE       /      /

**Scripture of the Day**

"Behold, he who has repented of his sins, the same is forgiven, and I, the Lord, remember them no more."

*Doctrine and Covenants 58:42*

**Quote of the Day**

"Because of God's perfect love for us and the eternal sacrifice of Jesus Christ, our sins—both great and small—can be blotted out and remembered no more. We can stand before Him pure, worthy, and sanctified."

*Dieter F. Uchtdorf, "God among Us," April 2021*

### HOW DID GOD SHOW UP FOR YOU TODAY?

### WHAT CAN YOU ASK CHRIST TO HELP YOU CARRY RIGHT NOW?

### WHAT IS YOUR HOPE FOR TOMORROW?

DATE    /    /

## Scripture of the Day
*Psalm 139:1–3*

"O Lord, thou hast searched me, and known me. Thou knowest my downsitting and mine uprising, thou understandest my thought afar off. Thou compassest my path and my lying down, and art acquainted with all my ways."

## Quote of the Day
*Ulisses Soares, "Seek Christ in Every Thought," October 2020*

"He truly knows every aspect of our souls. Being aware of all that is necessary for us in this life, the Savior invites us to seek Him in every thought and to follow Him with all our heart. This gives us the promise that we can walk in His light and that His guidance prevents the influence of darkness in our life. Seeking Christ in every thought and following Him with all our heart requires that we align our mind and desires with His."

### HOW DID GOD SHOW UP FOR YOU TODAY?

### WHAT CAN YOU ASK CHRIST TO HELP YOU CARRY RIGHT NOW?

### WHAT IS YOUR HOPE FOR TOMORROW?

DATE     /     /

## Scripture of the Day

*Matthew 20:18–19*

"Behold, we go up to Jerusalem; and the Son of man shall be betrayed unto the chief priests and unto the scribes, and they shall condemn him to death, and shall deliver him to the Gentiles to mock, and to scourge, and to crucify him: and the third day he shall rise again."

## Quote of the Day

*Dallin H. Oaks, "What Has Our Savior Done for Us?" April 2021*

"The Resurrection gives us the perspective and the strength to endure the mortal challenges faced by each of us and those we love. It gives us a new way to view the physical, mental, or emotional deficiencies we have at birth or acquire during mortal life. It gives us the strength to endure sorrows, failures, and frustrations. Because each of us has an assured resurrection, we know that these mortal deficiencies and oppositions are only temporary."

### HOW DID GOD SHOW UP FOR YOU TODAY?

### WHAT CAN YOU ASK CHRIST TO HELP YOU CARRY RIGHT NOW?

### WHAT IS YOUR HOPE FOR TOMORROW?

DATE  /  /

## Scripture of the Day

*John 3:16–17*

"For God so loved the world, that he gave his only begotten Son, that whosoever believeth in him should not perish, but have everlasting life. For God sent not his Son into the world to condemn the world; but that the world through him might be saved."

## Quote of the Day

*Russell M. Nelson, "Pure Truth, Pure Doctrine, and Pure Revelation," October 2021*

"The pure doctrine of Christ is powerful. It changes the life of everyone who understands it and seeks to implement it in his or her life. The doctrine of Christ helps us find and stay on the covenant path. Staying on that narrow but well-defined path will ultimately qualify us to receive all that God has. Nothing could be worth more than *all* our Father has!"

### HOW DID GOD SHOW UP FOR YOU TODAY?

### WHAT CAN YOU ASK CHRIST TO HELP YOU CARRY RIGHT NOW?

### WHAT IS YOUR HOPE FOR TOMORROW?

DATE      /      /

**Scripture of the Day**

"And Alma and his people did not raise their voices to the Lord their God, but did pour out their hearts to him; and he did know the thoughts of their hearts."

*Mosiah 24:12*

**Quote of the Day**

"I can't go at it alone, and I don't need to, and I won't. Choosing to be bound to my Savior, Jesus Christ, through the covenants I have made with God, 'I can do all things through Christ which strengtheneth me.' Covenant keepers are blessed with the Savior's relief."

*Camille N. Johnson, "Jesus Christ Is Relief," April 2023*

### HOW DID GOD SHOW UP FOR YOU TODAY?

### WHAT CAN YOU ASK CHRIST TO HELP YOU CARRY RIGHT NOW?

### WHAT IS YOUR HOPE FOR TOMORROW?

DATE      /      /

## *Scripture of the Day*

*Moroni 7:47*

"But charity is the pure love of Christ, and it endureth forever; and whoso is found possessed of it at the last day, it shall be well with him."

## *Quote of the Day*

*Russell M. Nelson, "Peacemakers Needed," April 2023*

"Charity is the antidote to contention. Charity is the spiritual gift that helps us to cast off the natural man, who is selfish, defensive, prideful, and jealous. Charity is the principal characteristic of a true follower of Jesus Christ. Charity defines a peacemaker."

### HOW DID GOD SHOW UP FOR YOU TODAY?

### WHAT CAN YOU ASK CHRIST TO HELP YOU CARRY RIGHT NOW?

### WHAT IS YOUR HOPE FOR TOMORROW?

DATE      /      /

## Scripture of the Day

*Doctrine and Covenants 19:16–19*

"For behold, I, God, have suffered these things for all, that they might not suffer if they would repent; but if they would not repent they must suffer even as I; which suffering caused myself, even God, the greatest of all, to tremble because of pain, and to bleed at every pore, and to suffer both body and spirit—and would that I might not drink the bitter cup, and shrink—nevertheless, glory be to the Father, and I partook and finished my preparations unto the children of men."

## Quote of the Day

*Carl B. Cook, "Just Keep Going—with Faith," April 2023*

"Thankfully, when we are weak or incapable, the Lord can strengthen our faith. He can increase our capacity beyond our own."

### HOW DID GOD SHOW UP FOR YOU TODAY?

### WHAT CAN YOU ASK CHRIST TO HELP YOU CARRY RIGHT NOW?

### WHAT IS YOUR HOPE FOR TOMORROW?

DATE      /      /

## *Scripture of the Day*

Psalm 34:18, 22

"The Lord is nigh unto them that are of a broken heart; and saveth such as be of a contrite spirit. . . . The Lord redeemeth the soul of his servants: and none of them that trust in him shall be desolate."

## *Quote of the Day*

Bonnie H. Cordon, "Come unto Christ and Don't Come Alone," October 2021

"We continually seek to draw closer to the Savior through faith, cherished repentance, and keeping the commandments. As we bind ourselves to Him through covenants and ordinances, our lives are filled with confidence, protection, and deep and lasting joy."

### HOW DID GOD SHOW UP FOR YOU TODAY?

### WHAT CAN YOU ASK CHRIST TO HELP YOU CARRY RIGHT NOW?

### WHAT IS YOUR HOPE FOR TOMORROW?

DATE    /    /

## Scripture of the Day

"And immediately he rose up before them, and took up that whereon he lay, and departed to his own house, glorifying God."

*Luke 5:25*

## Quote of the Day

*Camille N. Johnson, "Jesus Christ Is Relief," April 2023*

"Jesus Christ had provided the hoped-for healing—physical *relief* from pain and the crippling consequences of chronic disease. Significantly, the Savior also provided spiritual *relief* in cleansing the man from sin. And the friends—in their efforts to care for one in need, they found the source of relief; they found Jesus Christ. I testify that Jesus Christ *is* relief. Through the Atonement of Jesus Christ, we may be relieved of the burden and consequences of sin and be succored in our infirmities."

### HOW DID GOD SHOW UP FOR YOU TODAY?

### WHAT CAN YOU ASK CHRIST TO HELP YOU CARRY RIGHT NOW?

### WHAT IS YOUR HOPE FOR TOMORROW?

DATE    /    /

**Scripture of the Day**

"Let us therefore come boldly unto the throne of grace, that we may obtain mercy, and find grace to help in time of need."

*Hebrews 4:16*

**Quote of the Day**

"The gift of repentance is an expression of God's kindness toward His children, and it is a demonstration of His incomparable power to help us overcome the sins we commit. It is also an evidence of the patience and long-suffering our loving Father has for our mortal weakness and frailties."

*Ulisses Soares, "Jesus Christ: The Caregiver of Our Soul," April 2021*

HOW DID GOD SHOW UP FOR YOU TODAY?

WHAT CAN YOU ASK CHRIST TO HELP YOU CARRY RIGHT NOW?

WHAT IS YOUR HOPE FOR TOMORROW?

DATE    /    /

## Scripture of the Day

*Jacob 7:5*

"For I truly had seen angels, and they had ministered unto me. And also, I had heard the voice of the Lord speaking unto me in very word, from time to time; wherefore, I could not be shaken."

## Quote of the Day

*Anthony D. Perkins, "Remember Thy Suffering Saints, O Lord," October 2021*

"I vividly recall my own experience at one point in my cancer battle when the doctors had not yet diagnosed the cause of some severe pain. I sat with my wife, intending to offer a routine blessing on our lunch. Instead, all I could do was simply weep, 'Heavenly Father, please help me. I am so sick.' For the next 20 to 30 seconds, I was encircled in His love. I was given no reason for my illness, no indication of the ultimate outcome, and no relief from the pain. I just felt of His pure love, and that was and is enough."

### HOW DID GOD SHOW UP FOR YOU TODAY?

### WHAT CAN YOU ASK CHRIST TO HELP YOU CARRY RIGHT NOW?

### WHAT IS YOUR HOPE FOR TOMORROW?

DATE        /       /

## Scripture of the Day

*Mosiah 4:10*

"And again, believe that ye must repent of your sins and forsake them, and humble yourselves before God; and ask in sincerity of heart that he would forgive you; and now, if you believe all these things see that ye do them."

## Quote of the Day

*Russell M. Nelson, "Welcome Message," April 2021*

"The gospel of Jesus Christ is a gospel of repentance. Because of the Savior's Atonement, His gospel provides an invitation to keep changing, growing, and becoming more pure. It is a gospel of hope, of healing, and of progress. Thus, the gospel is a message of *joy*! Our spirits rejoice with every small step forward we take."

### HOW DID GOD SHOW UP FOR YOU TODAY?

### WHAT CAN YOU ASK CHRIST TO HELP YOU CARRY RIGHT NOW?

### WHAT IS YOUR HOPE FOR TOMORROW?

DATE     /     /

## Scripture of the Day

"And whoso receiveth you, there I will be also, for I will go before your face. I will be on your right hand and on your left, and my Spirit shall be in your hearts, and mine angels round about you, to bear you up."

*Doctrine and Covenants 84:88*

## Quote of the Day

"When it comes to your happiness and salvation, it is always worth the effort to keep trying. It is worth the effort to adjust your lifestyle and traditions. The Lord is aware of the challenges you face. He knows you, He loves you, and I promise, He will send angels to help you."

*Carlos A. Godoy, "I Believe in Angels," October 2020*

### HOW DID GOD SHOW UP FOR YOU TODAY?

### WHAT CAN YOU ASK CHRIST TO HELP YOU CARRY RIGHT NOW?

### WHAT IS YOUR HOPE FOR TOMORROW?

DATE      /      /

## Scripture of the Day

*Psalm 136:1, 4, 25–26*

"O give thanks unto the Lord; for he is good: for his mercy endureth for ever. . . . To him who alone doeth great wonders: for his mercy endureth for ever. . . . Who giveth food to all flesh: for his mercy endureth for ever. O give thanks unto the God of heaven: for his mercy endureth for ever."

## Quote of the Day

*D. Todd Christofferson, "The Love of God," October 2021*

"Our Heavenly Father loves us profoundly and perfectly. In His love, He created a plan, a plan of redemption and happiness to open to us all the opportunities and joys we are willing to receive, up to and including all that He has and is. To achieve this, He was even willing to offer His Beloved Son, Jesus Christ, as our Redeemer. . . . His is a Father's pure love—universal to all yet personal to each."

### HOW DID GOD SHOW UP FOR YOU TODAY?

### WHAT CAN YOU ASK CHRIST TO HELP YOU CARRY RIGHT NOW?

### WHAT IS YOUR HOPE FOR TOMORROW?

DATE        /        /

## *Scripture of the Day*

*Mosiah 7:33*

"But if ye will turn to the Lord with full purpose of heart, and put your trust in him, and serve him with all diligence of mind, if ye do this, he will, according to his own will and pleasure, deliver you out of bondage."

## *Quote of the Day*

*Dale G. Renlund, "Latter-day Saints Keep on Trying," April 2015*

"Even if we've been a conscious, deliberate sinner or have repeatedly faced failure and disappointment, the moment we decide to try again, the Atonement of Christ can help us. And we need to remember that it is not the Holy Ghost that tells us we're so far gone that we might as well give up."

### HOW DID GOD SHOW UP FOR YOU TODAY?

### WHAT CAN YOU ASK CHRIST TO HELP YOU CARRY RIGHT NOW?

### WHAT IS YOUR HOPE FOR TOMORROW?

DATE    /    /

## *Scripture of the Day*

*Acts 10:38*

"How God anointed Jesus of Nazareth with the Holy Ghost and with power: who went about doing good, and healing all that were oppressed of the devil; for God was with him."

## *Quote of the Day*

*M. Russell Ballard, "Watch Ye Therefore, and Pray Always," October 2020*

"The Savior prayed and then He 'went about doing good' by feeding the poor, providing courage and support to those in need, and reaching out in love, forgiveness, peace, and rest to all who would come unto Him. He continues to reach out to us."

### HOW DID GOD SHOW UP FOR YOU TODAY?

### WHAT CAN YOU ASK CHRIST TO HELP YOU CARRY RIGHT NOW?

### WHAT IS YOUR HOPE FOR TOMORROW?

DATE     /     /

## *Scripture of the Day*

3 Nephi 11:14

"Arise and come forth unto me, that ye may thrust your hands into my side, and also that ye may feel the prints of the nails in my hands and in my feet, that ye may know that I am the God of Israel, and the God of the whole earth, and have been slain for the sins of the world."

## *Quote of the Day*

Bonnie H. Cordon, "Never Give Up an Opportunity to Testify of Christ," April 2023

"When Christ physically visited the Nephites at their temple, His invitation was not to stand at a distance and look upon Him, but to touch Him, to feel for themselves the reality of the Savior of humankind. How can we draw close enough to gain a personal witness of Jesus Christ?"

#### HOW DID GOD SHOW UP FOR YOU TODAY?

#### WHAT CAN YOU ASK CHRIST TO HELP YOU CARRY RIGHT NOW?

#### WHAT IS YOUR HOPE FOR TOMORROW?

DATE    /    /

## Scripture of the Day

*Helaman 3:35*

"Nevertheless they did fast and pray oft, and did wax stronger and stronger in their humility, and firmer and firmer in the faith of Christ, unto the filling their souls with joy and consolation, yea, even to the purifying and the sanctification of their hearts, which sanctification cometh because of their yielding their hearts unto God."

## Quote of the Day

*Russell M. Nelson, "Peacemakers Needed," April 2023*

"If you are serious about helping to gather Israel and about building relationships that will last throughout the eternities, now is the time to lay aside bitterness. *Now* is the time to cease insisting that it is your way or no way. *Now* is the time to stop doing things that make others walk on eggshells for fear of upsetting you. *Now* is the time to bury your weapons of war. If your verbal arsenal is filled with insults and accusations, *now* is the time to put them away. You will arise as a spiritually strong man or woman of Christ."

### HOW DID GOD SHOW UP FOR YOU TODAY?

### WHAT CAN YOU ASK CHRIST TO HELP YOU CARRY RIGHT NOW?

### WHAT IS YOUR HOPE FOR TOMORROW?

DATE    /    /

## Scripture of the Day

*Doctrine and Covenants 18:19*

"And if you have not faith, hope, and charity, you can do nothing."

## Quote of the Day

*Dieter F. Uchtdorf, "Our Heartfelt All," April 2022*

"Jesus taught that our offering may be large or it may be small, but either way, it must be our *heartfelt all*."

### HOW DID GOD SHOW UP FOR YOU TODAY?

### WHAT CAN YOU ASK CHRIST TO HELP YOU CARRY RIGHT NOW?

### WHAT IS YOUR HOPE FOR TOMORROW?

DATE    /    /

## Scripture of the Day

"Wherewith shall I come before the Lord, and bow myself before the high God? shall I come before him with burnt offerings, with calves of a year old?"

*Micah 6:6*

## Quote of the Day

"Without the blessings that come from Heavenly Father and Jesus Christ, we can never do enough or be enough by ourselves. The good news, though, is that because of and through Jesus Christ we can become enough. All people will be saved from physical death by the grace of God, through the death and Resurrection of Jesus Christ. . . . God delights in mercy and does not begrudge its use."

*Dale G. Renlund, "Do Justly, Love Mercy, and Walk Humbly with God," October 2020*

### HOW DID GOD SHOW UP FOR YOU TODAY?

### WHAT CAN YOU ASK CHRIST TO HELP YOU CARRY RIGHT NOW?

### WHAT IS YOUR HOPE FOR TOMORROW?

DATE     /     /

**Scripture of the Day**

———

*John 12:12–13*

"On the next day much people that were come to the feast, when they heard that Jesus was coming to Jerusalem, took branches of palm trees, and went forth to meet him, and cried, Hosanna: Blessed is the King of Israel that cometh in the name of the Lord."

**Quote of the Day**

———

*Dallin H. Oaks, "What Has Our Savior Done for Us?" April 2021*

"As part of the Father's plan, the Resurrection of Jesus Christ overcame death to assure each of us immortality. Jesus Christ's atoning sacrifice gives each of us the opportunity to repent of our sins and return clean to our heavenly home. His commandments and covenants show us the way, and His priesthood gives the authority to perform the ordinances that are essential to reach that destiny. And our Savior willingly experienced all mortal pains and infirmities that He would know how to strengthen us in our afflictions. Jesus Christ did all of this because He loves all of the children of God. Love is the motivation for it all, and it was so from the very beginning."

### HOW DID GOD SHOW UP FOR YOU TODAY?

### WHAT CAN YOU ASK CHRIST TO HELP YOU CARRY RIGHT NOW?

### WHAT IS YOUR HOPE FOR TOMORROW?

DATE    /    /

## Scripture of the Day

*1 Corinthians 13:4–5*

"Charity suffereth long, and is kind; charity envieth not; charity vaunteth not itself, is not puffed up, doth not behave itself unseemly, seeketh not her own, is not easily provoked, thinketh no evil."

## Quote of the Day

*Mark A. Bragg, "Christlike Poise," April 2023*

"Poise is not spoken about much these days and practiced even less in turbulent and divisive times. . . . Spiritual poise blesses us to stay calm and focused on what matters most, especially when we are under pressure."

### HOW DID GOD SHOW UP FOR YOU TODAY?

### WHAT CAN YOU ASK CHRIST TO HELP YOU CARRY RIGHT NOW?

### WHAT IS YOUR HOPE FOR TOMORROW?

DATE      /      /

## Scripture of the Day

*Alma 33:23*

"And now, my brethren, I desire that ye shall plant this word in your hearts, and as it beginneth to swell even so nourish it by your faith. And behold, it will become a tree, springing up in you unto everlasting life. And then may God grant unto you that your burdens may be light, through the joy of his Son. And even all this can ye do if ye will."

## Quote of the Day

*David A. Bednar, "Abide in Me, and I in You; Therefore Walk with Me," April 2023*

"The seed we should strive to plant in our hearts is the word—even the life, mission, and doctrine of Jesus Christ. And as the word is nourished by faith, it can become a tree springing up *in us* unto everlasting life."

### HOW DID GOD SHOW UP FOR YOU TODAY?

### WHAT CAN YOU ASK CHRIST TO HELP YOU CARRY RIGHT NOW?

### WHAT IS YOUR HOPE FOR TOMORROW?

DATE     /     /

## Scripture of the Day

*Ether 12:41*

"And now, I would commend you to seek this Jesus of whom the prophets and apostles have written, that the grace of God the Father, and also the Lord Jesus Christ, and the Holy Ghost, which beareth record of them, may be and abide in you forever."

## Quote of the Day

*Russell M. Nelson, "The Temple and Your Spiritual Foundation," October 2021*

"God, our Heavenly Father, wants *you* to choose to come home to Him. His plan of eternal progression is not complicated, and it honors your agency. You are free to choose who you will be—and with whom you will be—in the world to come! God lives! Jesus is the Christ! This is His Church, restored to help you fulfill your divine destiny."

### HOW DID GOD SHOW UP FOR YOU TODAY?

### WHAT CAN YOU ASK CHRIST TO HELP YOU CARRY RIGHT NOW?

### WHAT IS YOUR HOPE FOR TOMORROW?

DATE      /      /

## Scripture of the Day

*Doctrine and Covenants 14:7*

"And, if you keep my commandments and endure to the end you shall have eternal life, which gift is the greatest of all the gifts of God."

## Quote of the Day

*Neil L. Andersen, "My Mind Caught Hold upon This Thought of Jesus Christ," April 2023*

"Remember, you are a spirit child of Heavenly Father. As the Apostle Paul explains, we are 'the offspring of God.' You have lived with your own individual identity long before coming to earth. Our Father created a perfect plan for us to come to earth, learn, and return to Him. He sent His Beloved Son that through the power of His infinite Atonement and Resurrection, we live beyond the grave; and as we are willing to exercise faith in Him and repent of our sins, we are forgiven and receive the hope of eternal life."

### HOW DID GOD SHOW UP FOR YOU TODAY?

### WHAT CAN YOU ASK CHRIST TO HELP YOU CARRY RIGHT NOW?

### WHAT IS YOUR HOPE FOR TOMORROW?

DATE      /      /

## *Scripture of the Day*

"Sing unto the Lord; for he hath done excellent things: this is known in all the earth. Cry out and shout, thou inhabitant of Zion: for great is the Holy One of Israel in the midst of thee."

*Isaiah 12:5–6*

## *Quote of the Day*

*Susan H. Porter, "God's Love: The Most Joyous to the Soul," October 2021*

"God's love is not found in the *circumstances* of our lives but in His *presence* in our lives. We know of His love when we receive strength beyond our own and when His Spirit brings peace, comfort, and direction. At times it may be difficult to feel His love. We can pray to have our eyes opened to see His hand in our lives and to see His love in the beauty of His creations."

### HOW DID GOD SHOW UP FOR YOU TODAY?

### WHAT CAN YOU ASK CHRIST TO HELP YOU CARRY RIGHT NOW?

### WHAT IS YOUR HOPE FOR TOMORROW?

DATE        /        /

## Scripture of the Day

"He that spared not his own Son, but delivered him up for us all, how shall he not with him also freely give us all things?"

*Romans 8:32*

## Quote of the Day

"Nothing can separate us from the love of God. Remembering this love can help you push back the confusion of the world that tries to weaken your confidence in your divine identity and blind you of your potential."

*Bonnie H. Cordon, "Come unto Christ and Don't Come Alone," October 2021*

### HOW DID GOD SHOW UP FOR YOU TODAY?

### WHAT CAN YOU ASK CHRIST TO HELP YOU CARRY RIGHT NOW?

### WHAT IS YOUR HOPE FOR TOMORROW?

DATE ____ / ____ / ____

**Scripture of the Day**
———
*John 1:5*

"And the light shineth in darkness; and the darkness comprehended it not."

**Quote of the Day**
———
*Timothy J. Dyches, "Light Cleaveth unto Light," April 2021*

"I testify that Jesus Christ is the everlasting light that 'shineth in darkness.' There is no darkness that can ever suppress, extinguish, overpower, or defeat that light. Our Heavenly Father freely offers that light to you. You are never alone. He hears and answers every prayer."

### HOW DID GOD SHOW UP FOR YOU TODAY?

### WHAT CAN YOU ASK CHRIST TO HELP YOU CARRY RIGHT NOW?

### WHAT IS YOUR HOPE FOR TOMORROW?

DATE     /     /

## Scripture of the Day
*Moroni 7:22*

"For behold, God knowing all things, being from everlasting to everlasting, behold, he sent angels to minister unto the children of men, to make manifest concerning the coming of Christ; and in Christ there should come every good thing."

## Quote of the Day
*Camille N. Johnson, "Invite Christ to Author Your Story," October 2021*

"Frankly, few of us would probably write into our stories the trials that refine us. But don't we love the glorious culmination of a story we read when the protagonist overcomes the struggle? Trials are the elements of the plot that make our favorite stories compelling, timeless, faith promoting, and worthy of telling. The beautiful struggles written into *our* stories are what draw us closer to the Savior and refine us, making us more like Him."

### HOW DID GOD SHOW UP FOR YOU TODAY?

### WHAT CAN YOU ASK CHRIST TO HELP YOU CARRY RIGHT NOW?

### WHAT IS YOUR HOPE FOR TOMORROW?

DATE      /      /

## *Scripture of the Day*

"Cleave unto God as he cleaveth unto you."

*Jacob 6:5*

## *Quote of the Day*

*Russell M. Nelson, "What We Are Learning and Will Never Forget," April 2021*

"Amid the *losses* we have experienced, there are also some things we have *found*. Some have found deeper faith in our Heavenly Father and His Son, Jesus Christ. Many have found a fresh perspective on life—even an eternal perspective. You may have found stronger relationships with your loved ones and with the Lord. I hope you have found an increased ability to *hear Him* and receive personal revelation. Difficult trials often provide opportunities to grow that would not have come in any other way."

### HOW DID GOD SHOW UP FOR YOU TODAY?

### WHAT CAN YOU ASK CHRIST TO HELP YOU CARRY RIGHT NOW?

### WHAT IS YOUR HOPE FOR TOMORROW?

DATE     /     /

## *Scripture of the Day*

*Doctrine and Covenants 109:14–15*

"And do thou grant, Holy Father, that all those who shall worship in this house may be taught words of wisdom out of the best books, and that they may seek learning even by study, and also by faith, as thou hast said; and that they may grow up in thee, and receive a fulness of the Holy Ghost, and be organized according to thy laws, and be prepared to obtain every needful thing."

## *Quote of the Day*

*Dale G. Renlund, "Accessing God's Power through Covenants," April 2023*

"As you walk the covenant path, from baptism to the temple and throughout life, I promise you power to go against the natural worldly flow—power to learn, power to repent and be sanctified, and power to find hope, comfort, and even joy as you face life's challenges. I promise you and your family protection against the influence of the adversary, especially when you make the temple a major focus in your life."

### HOW DID GOD SHOW UP FOR YOU TODAY?

### WHAT CAN YOU ASK CHRIST TO HELP YOU CARRY RIGHT NOW?

### WHAT IS YOUR HOPE FOR TOMORROW?

DATE    /    /

## *Scripture of the Day*

*Numbers 6:24–27*

"The Lord bless thee, and keep thee: The Lord make his face shine upon thee, and be gracious unto thee: The Lord lift up his countenance upon thee, and give thee peace. And they shall put my name upon the children of Israel; and I will bless them."

## *Quote of the Day*

*Dieter F. Uchtdorf, "God among Us," April 2021*

"Suppose Jesus came to your ward, to your branch, or to your home today. What would that be like? He would see right into your heart. Outward appearances would lose their importance. He would know you as you are. He would know your heart's desires. . . . One look into His eyes and we would never be the same. We would be forever changed. Transformed by the profound realization that, indeed, God is among us."

### HOW DID GOD SHOW UP FOR YOU TODAY?

### WHAT CAN YOU ASK CHRIST TO HELP YOU CARRY RIGHT NOW?

### WHAT IS YOUR HOPE FOR TOMORROW?

DATE      /      /

**Scripture of the Day**

"That there should be no schism in the body; but that the members should have the same care one for another."

*1 Corinthians 12:25*

**Quote of the Day**

"Unity does not mean simply agreeing that everyone should do his or her own thing or go his or her own way. We cannot be one unless we all bend our efforts to the common cause."

*D. Todd Christofferson, "One in Christ," April 2023*

### HOW DID GOD SHOW UP FOR YOU TODAY?

### WHAT CAN YOU ASK CHRIST TO HELP YOU CARRY RIGHT NOW?

### WHAT IS YOUR HOPE FOR TOMORROW?

DATE    /    /

## Scripture of the Day

"With men it is impossible, but not with God: for with God all things are possible."

*Mark 10:27*

## Quote of the Day

"God did part the Red Sea, and He did give us the Book of Mormon. He can heal us of our sins, and He can and will bless us, His children, in our daily lives. I know that He lives and loves us and is today a God of miracles."

*Sydney S. Reynolds,*
*"A God of Miracles,"*
*April 2001*

### HOW DID GOD SHOW UP FOR YOU TODAY?

### WHAT CAN YOU ASK CHRIST TO HELP YOU CARRY RIGHT NOW?

### WHAT IS YOUR HOPE FOR TOMORROW?

DATE    /    /

## Scripture of the Day

*Alma 22:15*

"And it came to pass that after Aaron had expounded these things unto him, the king said: What shall I do that I may have this eternal life of which thou hast spoken? Yea, what shall I do that I may be born of God, having this wicked spirit rooted out of my breast, and receive his Spirit, that I may be filled with joy, that I may not be cast off at the last day? Behold, said he, I will give up all that I possess, yea, I will forsake my kingdom, that I may receive this great joy."

## Quote of the Day

*Craig C. Christensen, "There Can Be Nothing So Exquisite and Sweet as Was My Joy" April 2023*

"The joy we speak of is a gift for the faithful, yet it comes with a price. Joy is not cheap or casually given. Rather, it is bought 'with the precious blood of [Jesus] Christ.' If we really understood the value of true, godly joy, we would not hesitate to sacrifice any worldly possession or make any necessary life changes to receive it."

### HOW DID GOD SHOW UP FOR YOU TODAY?

### WHAT CAN YOU ASK CHRIST TO HELP YOU CARRY RIGHT NOW?

### WHAT IS YOUR HOPE FOR TOMORROW?

DATE      /      /

## *Scripture of the Day*

*3 Nephi 9:13–14*

"O all ye that are spared because ye were more righteous than they, will ye not now return unto me, and repent of your sins, and be converted, that I may heal you? Yea, verily I say unto you, if ye will come unto me ye shall have eternal life. Behold, mine arm of mercy is extended towards you, and whosoever will come, him will I receive; and blessed are those who come unto me."

## *Quote of the Day*

*Russell M. Nelson, "The Answer Is Always Jesus Christ," April 2023*

"Jesus Christ extends that same invitation to you today. I plead with you to come unto Him so that He can heal *you*! He will heal you from sin as you repent. He will heal you from sadness and fear. He will heal you from the wounds of this world."

### HOW DID GOD SHOW UP FOR YOU TODAY?

### WHAT CAN YOU ASK CHRIST TO HELP YOU CARRY RIGHT NOW?

### WHAT IS YOUR HOPE FOR TOMORROW?

DATE     /     /

## Scripture of the Day

*Doctrine and Covenants 88:125*

"And above all things, clothe yourselves with the bond of charity, as with a mantle, which is the bond of perfectness and peace."

## Quote of the Day

*Ulisses Soares, "Followers of the Prince of Peace," April 2023*

"During His earthly ministry, the Savior's teachings focused—not only, but particularly—on the virtues of love, charity, patience, humility, and compassion—fundamental attributes to those who want to become closer to Him and promote His peace. Such attributes are gifts from God, and as we strive to develop them, we will begin to see our neighbor's differences and weaknesses with more empathy, sensitivity, respect, and tolerance."

### HOW DID GOD SHOW UP FOR YOU TODAY?

### WHAT CAN YOU ASK CHRIST TO HELP YOU CARRY RIGHT NOW?

### WHAT IS YOUR HOPE FOR TOMORROW?

DATE    /    /

### Scripture of the Day

"For I know the thoughts that I think toward you, saith the Lord, thoughts of peace, and not of evil, to give you an expected end."

*Jeremiah 29:11*

### Quote of the Day

"Our Savior, Jesus Christ, knows everything about us we don't want anyone else to know, and He still loves us. His is a gospel of second and third chances, made possible by His atoning sacrifice."

*Gerrit W. Gong, "Room in the Inn," April 2021*

## HOW DID GOD SHOW UP FOR YOU TODAY?

## WHAT CAN YOU ASK CHRIST TO HELP YOU CARRY RIGHT NOW?

## WHAT IS YOUR HOPE FOR TOMORROW?

DATE    /    /

## Scripture of the Day

*John 14:20*

"At that day ye shall know that I am in my Father, and ye in me, and I in you."

## Quote of the Day

*Henry B. Eyring, "Finding Personal Peace," April 2023*

"First, the gift of peace is given *after* we have the faith to keep His commandments. For those who are covenant members of the Lord's Church, obedience is what we have already promised to do. Second, the Holy Ghost will come and abide with us. The Lord says that as we continue to be faithful, the Holy Ghost will dwell in us. That is the promise in the sacramental prayer that the Spirit will be our companion and that we will feel, in our hearts and minds, His comfort."

### HOW DID GOD SHOW UP FOR YOU TODAY?

### WHAT CAN YOU ASK CHRIST TO HELP YOU CARRY RIGHT NOW?

### WHAT IS YOUR HOPE FOR TOMORROW?

DATE    /    /

## Scripture of the Day

"And let us not be weary in well doing: for in due season we shall reap, if we faint not."

*Galatians 6:9*

## Quote of the Day

"I testify you are beloved. The Lord knows how hard you are trying."

*Sharon Eubank, "Christ: The Light that Shines in Darkness," April 2019*

### HOW DID GOD SHOW UP FOR YOU TODAY?

### WHAT CAN YOU ASK CHRIST TO HELP YOU CARRY RIGHT NOW?

### WHAT IS YOUR HOPE FOR TOMORROW?

DATE    /    /

## Scripture of the Day

*Alma 34:15–16*

"And thus he shall bring salvation to all those who shall believe on his name; this being the intent of this last sacrifice, to bring about the bowels of mercy, which overpowereth justice, and bringeth about means unto men that they may have faith unto repentance. And thus mercy can satisfy the demands of justice, and encircles them in the arms of safety, while he that exercises no faith unto repentance is exposed to the whole law of the demands of justice; therefore only unto him that has faith unto repentance is brought about the great and eternal plan of redemption."

## Quote of the Day

*Camille N. Johnson, "Jesus Christ Is Relief," April 2023*

"Repentance, through the Atonement of Jesus Christ, is what relieves us of the weight of the rocks of sin. And by this exquisite gift, God's mercy relieves us from the heavy and otherwise insurmountable demands of justice. The Atonement of Jesus Christ also makes it possible for us to receive strength to forgive, which allows us to unload the weight we carry because of mistreatment by others."

### HOW DID GOD SHOW UP FOR YOU TODAY?

### WHAT CAN YOU ASK CHRIST TO HELP YOU CARRY RIGHT NOW?

### WHAT IS YOUR HOPE FOR TOMORROW?

DATE        /        /

## Scripture of the Day

*Mosiah 24:15*

"And now it came to pass that the burdens which were laid upon Alma and his brethren were made light; yea, the Lord did strengthen them that they could bear up their burdens with ease, and they did submit cheerfully and with patience to all the will of the Lord."

## Quote of the Day

*Isaac K. Morrison, "We Can Do Hard Things through Him," October 2022*

"We can be of good cheer and be filled with peace in our tough times. The love we feel because of the Savior and His Atonement becomes a powerful resource to us in our trying moments."

### HOW DID GOD SHOW UP FOR YOU TODAY?

### WHAT CAN YOU ASK CHRIST TO HELP YOU CARRY RIGHT NOW?

### WHAT IS YOUR HOPE FOR TOMORROW?

DATE      /      /

**Scripture of the Day**

1 Nephi 17:49–51

"For God had commanded me that I should build a ship. . . . If God had commanded me to do all things I could do them. . . . And now, if the Lord has such great power, and has wrought so many miracles among the children of men, how is it that he cannot instruct me, that I should build a ship?"

**Quote of the Day**

Russell M. Nelson, "The Power of Spiritual Momentum," April 2022

"Do the spiritual work to seek miracles. Prayerfully ask God to help you exercise that kind of faith. . . . Few things will accelerate your spiritual momentum more than realizing the Lord is helping you to move a mountain in your life."

### HOW DID GOD SHOW UP FOR YOU TODAY?

### WHAT CAN YOU ASK CHRIST TO HELP YOU CARRY RIGHT NOW?

### WHAT IS YOUR HOPE FOR TOMORROW?

DATE      /      /

### Scripture of the Day

*Doctrine and Covenants 25:13*

"Wherefore, lift up thy heart and rejoice, and cleave unto the covenants which thou hast made."

### Quote of the Day

*Milton Camargo, "Focus on Jesus Christ," April 2023*

"Our covenants help us focus our attention, our thoughts, and our actions on Christ. As we 'cleave unto the covenants [we have] made,' we can more easily identify 'the things of this world' that we should 'lay aside' and 'the things of a better [world]' we should diligently seek. . . . This may mean that we have to change our vocabulary, using kinder words. It could mean replacing spiritually unhealthy habits with new habits that strengthen our relationship with the Lord, such as daily prayer and scripture study, individually and with our family."

**HOW DID GOD SHOW UP FOR YOU TODAY?**

**WHAT CAN YOU ASK CHRIST TO HELP YOU CARRY RIGHT NOW?**

**WHAT IS YOUR HOPE FOR TOMORROW?**

DATE    /    /

## *Scripture of the Day*

*Nahum 1:7*

"The Lord is good, a strong hold in the day of trouble; and he knoweth them that trust in him."

## *Quote of the Day*

*Camille N. Johnson, "Invite Christ to Author Your Story," October 2021*

"With a desire to let God prevail, with an ear to the Holy Ghost and a willingness to let the Savior be the author and finisher of his story, the boy David defeated Goliath and saved his people."

### HOW DID GOD SHOW UP FOR YOU TODAY?

### WHAT CAN YOU ASK CHRIST TO HELP YOU CARRY RIGHT NOW?

### WHAT IS YOUR HOPE FOR TOMORROW?

DATE        /         /

## *Scripture of the Day*

*1 Peter 5:6–7*

"Humble yourselves therefore under the mighty hand of God, that he may exalt you in due time: Casting all your care upon him; for he careth for you."

## *Quote of the Day*

*D. Todd Christofferson, "The Love of God," October 2021*

"Because They love you, They want you to have joy and success. Because They love you, They want you to repent because that is the path to happiness. But it is your choice—They honor your agency. You must choose to love Them, to serve Them, to keep Their commandments. Then They can more abundantly *bless* you as well as *love* you."

### HOW DID GOD SHOW UP FOR YOU TODAY?

### WHAT CAN YOU ASK CHRIST TO HELP YOU CARRY RIGHT NOW?

### WHAT IS YOUR HOPE FOR TOMORROW?

DATE    /    /

## Scripture of the Day

*Matthew 28:19–20*

"Go ye therefore, and teach all nations, baptizing them in the name of the Father, and of the Son, and of the Holy Ghost: Teaching them to observe all things whatsoever I have commanded you: and, lo, I am with you alway, even unto the end of the world."

## Quote of the Day

*S. Mark Palmer, "Our Sorrow Shall Be Turned into Joy," April 2021*

"The resurrected Lord gave His Apostles the charge to testify of Him. As with our living Apostles today, they left behind worldly occupations and spent the rest of their lives boldly declaring that God had raised up this Jesus. Their powerful testimonies led to thousands accepting the invitation to be baptized."

### HOW DID GOD SHOW UP FOR YOU TODAY?

### WHAT CAN YOU ASK CHRIST TO HELP YOU CARRY RIGHT NOW?

### WHAT IS YOUR HOPE FOR TOMORROW?

DATE     /     /

### *Scripture of the Day*

*Alma 32:17–18*

"Yea, there are many who do say: If thou wilt show unto us a sign from heaven, then we shall know of a surety; then we shall believe. Now I ask, is this faith? Behold, I say unto you, Nay; for if a man knoweth a thing he hath no cause to believe, for he knoweth it."

### *Quote of the Day*

*Ciro Schmeil, "Faith to Act and Become," October 2021*

"Through prayer and scripture study, the Lord has always given me the strength to act and endure one more day, one more week, and to try one more time. Many times the answers did not come right away. I have questions that have not been answered yet, but I keep asking and studying, and I am happy that the Lord continues to give me the strength to act as I wait for answers."

#### HOW DID GOD SHOW UP FOR YOU TODAY?

#### WHAT CAN YOU ASK CHRIST TO HELP YOU CARRY RIGHT NOW?

#### WHAT IS YOUR HOPE FOR TOMORROW?

DATE     /     /

## Scripture of the Day

*Enos 1:7–8*

"And I said: Lord, how is it done? And he said unto me: Because of thy faith in Christ, whom thou hast never before heard nor seen. And many years pass away before he shall manifest himself in the flesh; wherefore, go to, thy faith hath made thee whole."

## Quote of the Day

*Henry B. Eyring, "Prayers of Faith," April 2020*

"When I pray with faith, I have the Savior as my advocate with the Father and I can feel that my prayer reaches heaven. Answers come. Blessings are received. There is peace and joy even in hard times."

### HOW DID GOD SHOW UP FOR YOU TODAY?

### WHAT CAN YOU ASK CHRIST TO HELP YOU CARRY RIGHT NOW?

### WHAT IS YOUR HOPE FOR TOMORROW?

DATE          /          /

## *Scripture of the Day*

*2 Nephi 31:19*

"And now, my beloved brethren, after ye have gotten into this strait and narrow path, I would ask if all is done? Behold, I say unto you, Nay; for ye have not come thus far save it were by the word of Christ with unshaken faith in him, relying wholly upon the merits of him who is mighty to save."

## **Quote of the Day**

*Russell M. Nelson, "We Can Do Better and Be Better," April 2019*

"When we choose to repent, we choose to change! We allow the Savior to transform us into the best version of ourselves. We choose to grow spiritually and receive joy—the joy of redemption in Him. We choose to become more like Jesus Christ!"

### HOW DID GOD SHOW UP FOR YOU TODAY?

### WHAT CAN YOU ASK CHRIST TO HELP YOU CARRY RIGHT NOW?

### WHAT IS YOUR HOPE FOR TOMORROW?

DATE    /    /

## Scripture of the Day

"Then the word of the Lord came unto me, saying, Before I formed thee in the belly I knew thee; and before thou camest forth out of the womb I sanctified thee, and I ordained thee a prophet unto the nations."

*Jeremiah 1:4–5*

## Quote of the Day

"Current conditions in the world have caused some to panic. As God's covenant children, we do not need to chase after this or that to know how to navigate through these troubled times. We do not need to fear. The doctrine and principles that we must follow to survive spiritually and endure physically are found in the words of a living prophet."

*Allen D. Haynie, "A Living Prophet for the Latter Days," April 2023*

### HOW DID GOD SHOW UP FOR YOU TODAY?

### WHAT CAN YOU ASK CHRIST TO HELP YOU CARRY RIGHT NOW?

### WHAT IS YOUR HOPE FOR TOMORROW?

DATE    /    /

## *Scripture of the Day*

*Doctrine and Covenants 121:7–9*

"My son, peace be unto thy soul; thine adversity and thine afflictions shall be but a small moment; and then, if thou endure it well, God shall exalt thee on high; thou shalt triumph over thy foes. Thy friends do stand by thee, and they shall hail thee again with warm hearts and friendly hands."

## *Quote of the Day*

*Michelle D. Craig, "Wholehearted," October 2022*

"When your faith, your family, or your future are challenged—when you wonder why life is so hard when you are doing your best to live the gospel—remember that the Lord told us to expect troubles. Troubles are part of the plan and do not mean you've been abandoned; they are part of what it means to be His."

### HOW DID GOD SHOW UP FOR YOU TODAY?

### WHAT CAN YOU ASK CHRIST TO HELP YOU CARRY RIGHT NOW?

### WHAT IS YOUR HOPE FOR TOMORROW?

DATE    /    /

### Scripture of the Day

*Psalm 40:1–3*

"I waited patiently for the Lord; and he inclined unto me, and heard my cry. He brought me up also out of an horrible pit, out of the miry clay, and set my feet upon a rock, and established my goings. And he hath put a new song in my mouth, even praise unto our God: many shall see it, and fear, and shall trust in the Lord."

### Quote of the Day

*Denelson Silva, "Courage to Proclaim the Truth," October 2022*

"The challenges of life can knock us down, but know that when we exercise faith in Jesus Christ, '[our] afflictions shall be but a small moment' in the grand scope of eternity. Please do not create a deadline for the end of your difficulties and challenges. Trust in Heavenly Father and do not give up, for if we do give up, we will never know how the end of our journey would have been in the kingdom of God."

## HOW DID GOD SHOW UP FOR YOU TODAY?

## WHAT CAN YOU ASK CHRIST TO HELP YOU CARRY RIGHT NOW?

## WHAT IS YOUR HOPE FOR TOMORROW?

DATE    /    /

## Scripture of the Day

*Galatians 5:22–23*

"But the fruit of the Spirit is love, joy, peace, longsuffering, gentleness, goodness, faith, meekness, temperance: against such there is no law."

## Quote of the Day

*Dale G. Renlund, "Infuriating Unfairness," April 2021*

"As we develop faith in Jesus Christ, we should also strive to become like Him. We then approach others with compassion and try to alleviate unfairness where we find it; we can try to make things right within our sphere of influence."

### HOW DID GOD SHOW UP FOR YOU TODAY?

### WHAT CAN YOU ASK CHRIST TO HELP YOU CARRY RIGHT NOW?

### WHAT IS YOUR HOPE FOR TOMORROW?

DATE     /     /

## Scripture of the Day

"Let us run with patience the race that is set before us, looking unto Jesus the author and finisher of our faith."

*Hebrews 12:1–2*

## Quote of the Day

"The answer to the simplest questions and to the most complex problems is always the same. The answer is Jesus Christ. Every solution is found in Him."

*Ryan K. Olsen, "The Answer Is Jesus," October 2022*

### HOW DID GOD SHOW UP FOR YOU TODAY?

### WHAT CAN YOU ASK CHRIST TO HELP YOU CARRY RIGHT NOW?

### WHAT IS YOUR HOPE FOR TOMORROW?

DATE    /    /

## Scripture of the Day

"Yea, and as often as my people repent will I forgive them their trespasses against me."

*Mosiah 26:30*

## Quote of the Day

"We don't have to attempt the impossible in trying to rationalize our sins away. And on the other hand, we don't have to attempt the impossible in erasing the effects of sin by our own merit alone. Ours is not a religion of rationalization nor a religion of perfectionism but a religion of redemption—redemption through Jesus Christ."

*D. Todd Christofferson, "The Love of God," October 2021*

### HOW DID GOD SHOW UP FOR YOU TODAY?

### WHAT CAN YOU ASK CHRIST TO HELP YOU CARRY RIGHT NOW?

### WHAT IS YOUR HOPE FOR TOMORROW?

DATE      /      /

## Scripture of the Day

"Angels speak by the power of the Holy Ghost; wherefore, they speak the words of Christ. Wherefore, I said unto you, feast upon the words of Christ; for behold, the words of Christ will tell you all things what ye should do."

*2 Nephi 32:3*

## Quote of the Day

"I testify of angels, both the heavenly and the mortal kind. In doing so I am testifying that God never leaves us alone, never leaves us unaided in the challenges that we face."

*Jeffrey R. Holland, "The Ministry of Angels," October 2008*

### HOW DID GOD SHOW UP FOR YOU TODAY?

### WHAT CAN YOU ASK CHRIST TO HELP YOU CARRY RIGHT NOW?

### WHAT IS YOUR HOPE FOR TOMORROW?

DATE        /        /

## Scripture of the Day

*Alma 32:16*

"Therefore, blessed are they who humble themselves without being compelled to be humble; or rather, in other words, blessed is he that believeth in the word of God, and is baptized without stubbornness of heart, yea, without being brought to know the word, or even compelled to know, before they will believe."

## Quote of the Day

*Russell M. Nelson, "The Power of Spiritual Momentum," April 2022*

"None of us can control nations or the actions of others or even members of our own families. But we can control ourselves. My call today, dear brothers and sisters, is to end conflicts that are raging in *your* heart, *your* home, and *your* life. Bury any and all inclinations to hurt others—whether those inclinations be a temper, a sharp tongue, or a resentment for someone who has hurt you. . . . It can be painfully difficult to let go of anger that feels so justified. It can seem impossible to forgive those whose destructive actions have hurt the innocent. And yet, the Savior admonished us to 'forgive all men.'"

### HOW DID GOD SHOW UP FOR YOU TODAY?

### WHAT CAN YOU ASK CHRIST TO HELP YOU CARRY RIGHT NOW?

### WHAT IS YOUR HOPE FOR TOMORROW?

DATE          /          /

## *Scripture of the Day*

*Doctrine and Covenants 87:8*

"Wherefore, stand ye in holy places, and be not moved, until the day of the Lord come; for behold, it cometh quickly, saith the Lord."

## *Quote of the Day*

*David A. Bednar, "We Will Prove Them Herewith," October 2020*

"Faithfulness is not foolishness or fanaticism. Rather, it is trusting and placing our confidence in Jesus Christ as our Savior, on His name, and in His promises. As we 'press forward with a steadfastness in Christ, having a perfect brightness of hope, and a love of God and of all men,' we are blessed with an eternal perspective and vision that stretches far beyond our limited mortal capacity."

### HOW DID GOD SHOW UP FOR YOU TODAY?

### WHAT CAN YOU ASK CHRIST TO HELP YOU CARRY RIGHT NOW?

### WHAT IS YOUR HOPE FOR TOMORROW?

DATE     /     /

**Scripture of the Day**

"God is our refuge and strength, a very present help in trouble."

*Psalm 46:1*

**Quote of the Day**

"Jesus Christ can lighten our load. Jesus Christ can lift our burdens. Jesus Christ provides a way for us to be relieved of the weight of sin. Jesus Christ is our relief."

*Camille N. Johnson, "Jesus Christ Is Relief," April 2023*

### HOW DID GOD SHOW UP FOR YOU TODAY?

### WHAT CAN YOU ASK CHRIST TO HELP YOU CARRY RIGHT NOW?

### WHAT IS YOUR HOPE FOR TOMORROW?

DATE      /      /

## Scripture of the Day

*Philippians 4:6–7*

"Be careful for nothing; but in every thing by prayer and supplication with thanksgiving let your requests be made known unto God. And the peace of God, which passeth all understanding, shall keep your hearts and minds through Christ Jesus."

## Quote of the Day

*Dallin H. Oaks, "What Has Our Savior Done for Us?" April 2021*

"Our Savior feels and knows our temptations, our struggles, our heartaches, and our sufferings, for He willingly experienced them all as part of His Atonement. . . . All who suffer any kind of mortal infirmities should remember that our Savior experienced that kind of pain also, and that through His Atonement, He offers each of us the strength to bear it."

### HOW DID GOD SHOW UP FOR YOU TODAY?

### WHAT CAN YOU ASK CHRIST TO HELP YOU CARRY RIGHT NOW?

### WHAT IS YOUR HOPE FOR TOMORROW?

DATE    /    /

## *Scripture of the Day*

*Mosiah 23:7*

"But he said unto them: Behold, it is not expedient that we should have a king; for thus saith the Lord: Ye shall not esteem one flesh above another, or one man shall not think himself above another; therefore I say unto you it is not expedient that ye should have a king."

## **Quote of the Day**

*Dale G. Renlund, "Do Justly, Love Mercy, and Walk Humbly with God," October 2020*

"Jesus Christ exemplified what it means to do justly and to love mercy. He freely associated with sinners, treating them honorably and with respect. He taught the joy of keeping God's commandments and sought to lift rather than condemn those who struggled. He did denounce those who faulted Him for ministering to people they deemed unworthy. Such self-righteousness offended Him and still does."

### HOW DID GOD SHOW UP FOR YOU TODAY?

### WHAT CAN YOU ASK CHRIST TO HELP YOU CARRY RIGHT NOW?

### WHAT IS YOUR HOPE FOR TOMORROW?

DATE   /   /

## Scripture of the Day

*Alma 36:3*

"Whosoever shall put their trust in God shall be supported in their trials, and their troubles, and their afflictions, and shall be lifted up at the last day."

## Quote of the Day

*Hugo Montoya, "The Eternal Principle of Love," October 2022*

"Adversity in our lives can cause doubt about the fulfillment of the promises that have been made to us. Please trust in our Father. He always keeps His promises, and we can learn what He wants to teach us."

### HOW DID GOD SHOW UP FOR YOU TODAY?

### WHAT CAN YOU ASK CHRIST TO HELP YOU CARRY RIGHT NOW?

### WHAT IS YOUR HOPE FOR TOMORROW?

DATE    /    /

## Scripture of the Day

"But behold I say unto you, love your enemies, bless them that curse you, do good to them that hate you, and pray for them who despitefully use you and persecute you."

*3 Nephi 12:44*

## Quote of the Day

"The Savior's message is clear: His *true* disciples build, lift, encourage, persuade, and inspire—no matter how difficult the situation. True disciples of Jesus Christ are peacemakers."

*Russell M. Nelson, "Peacemakers Needed," April 2023*

### HOW DID GOD SHOW UP FOR YOU TODAY?

### WHAT CAN YOU ASK CHRIST TO HELP YOU CARRY RIGHT NOW?

### WHAT IS YOUR HOPE FOR TOMORROW?

DATE    /    /

## Scripture of the Day

*Doctrine and Covenants 123:17*

"Therefore, dearly beloved brethren, let us cheerfully do all things that lie in our power; and then may we stand still, with the utmost assurance, to see the salvation of God, and for his arm to be revealed."

## Quote of the Day

*M. Russell Ballard, "Lovest Thou Me More Than These?" October 2021*

"We must always remember that our true happiness depends upon our relationship with God, with Jesus Christ, and with each other. One way to demonstrate our love is by joining family, friends, and neighbors in doing some small things to better serve each other. Do things that make this world a better place."

### HOW DID GOD SHOW UP FOR YOU TODAY?

### WHAT CAN YOU ASK CHRIST TO HELP YOU CARRY RIGHT NOW?

### WHAT IS YOUR HOPE FOR TOMORROW?

DATE     /     /

## Scripture of the Day

*2 Samuel 22:32–33*

"For who is God, save the Lord? and who is a rock, save our God? God is my strength and power: and he maketh my way perfect."

## Quote of the Day

*Henry B. Eyring,
"The Faith to Ask
and Then to Act,"
October 2021*

"It takes faith in Jesus Christ to serve others for Him. It takes faith to go out to teach His gospel and offer it to people who may not feel the voice of the Spirit or may even deny the reality of the message. But as we exercise our faith in Christ—and follow His living prophet—faith will increase across the world."

### HOW DID GOD SHOW UP FOR YOU TODAY?

### WHAT CAN YOU ASK CHRIST TO HELP YOU CARRY RIGHT NOW?

### WHAT IS YOUR HOPE FOR TOMORROW?

DATE    /    /

## Scripture of the Day

*1 Corinthians 15:58*

"Be ye steadfast, unmoveable, always abounding in the work of the Lord, forasmuch as ye know that your labour is not in vain in the Lord."

## Quote of the Day

*David A. Bednar, "Put On Thy Strength, O Zion," October 2022*

"God does not have a list of favorites to which we must hope our names will someday be added. He does not limit "the chosen" to a restricted few. Instead, *our* hearts, *our* desires, *our* honoring of sacred gospel covenants and ordinances, *our* obedience to the commandments, and, most importantly, the Savior's redeeming grace and mercy determine whether we are counted as one of God's chosen."

### HOW DID GOD SHOW UP FOR YOU TODAY?

### WHAT CAN YOU ASK CHRIST TO HELP YOU CARRY RIGHT NOW?

### WHAT IS YOUR HOPE FOR TOMORROW?

DATE       /       /

## *Scripture of the Day*

*Mosiah 18:21*

"And he commanded them that there should be no contention one with another, but that they should look forward with one eye, having one faith and one baptism, having their hearts knit together in unity and in love one towards another."

## *Quote of the Day*

*Henry B. Eyring, "Finding Personal Peace," April 2023*

"The rising generation will become the nurturers of the generation to follow. The multiplier effect will produce a miracle. It will spread and grow over time, and the Lord's kingdom on earth will be prepared and ready to greet Him with shouts of hosanna. There will be peace on earth."

### HOW DID GOD SHOW UP FOR YOU TODAY?

### WHAT CAN YOU ASK CHRIST TO HELP YOU CARRY RIGHT NOW?

### WHAT IS YOUR HOPE FOR TOMORROW?

DATE    /    /

## Scripture of the Day

*2 Nephi 4:17*

"Nevertheless, notwithstanding the great goodness of the Lord, in showing me his great and marvelous works, my heart exclaimeth: O wretched man that I am! Yea, my heart sorroweth because of my flesh; my soul grieveth because of mine iniquities."

## Quote of the Day

*John A. McCune, "Come unto Christ—Living as Latter-day Saints," April 2020*

"There will be times when we will not be able to see any way that a current situation will end well and might even express, as Nephi, 'My heart sorroweth because of my flesh.' There may be times that the only hope we have *is* in Jesus Christ. What a blessing to have that hope and trust in Him. Christ is the one who will always keep His promises. His rest is assured for all who come unto Him."

### HOW DID GOD SHOW UP FOR YOU TODAY?

### WHAT CAN YOU ASK CHRIST TO HELP YOU CARRY RIGHT NOW?

### WHAT IS YOUR HOPE FOR TOMORROW?

DATE      /      /

## *Scripture of the Day*

*Moroni 7:19*

"Wherefore, I beseech of you, brethren, that ye should search diligently in the light of Christ that ye may know good from evil; and if ye will lay hold upon every good thing, and condemn it not, ye certainly will be a child of Christ."

## *Quote of the Day*

*Russell M. Nelson, "Pure Truth, Pure Doctrine, and Pure Revelation," October 2021*

"Imagine how quickly the devastating conflicts throughout the world—and those in our individual lives—would be resolved if we all chose to follow Jesus Christ and heed His teachings."

### HOW DID GOD SHOW UP FOR YOU TODAY?

### WHAT CAN YOU ASK CHRIST TO HELP YOU CARRY RIGHT NOW?

### WHAT IS YOUR HOPE FOR TOMORROW?

DATE    /    /

## Scripture of the Day

*3 Nephi 12:14–16*

"Verily, verily, I say unto you, I give unto you to be the light of this people. A city that is set on a hill cannot be hid. Behold, do men light a candle and put it under a bushel? Nay, but on a candlestick, and it giveth light to all that are in the house; therefore let your light so shine before this people, that they may see your good works and glorify your Father who is in heaven."

## Quote of the Day

*Marcus B. Nash, "Hold Up Your Light," October 2021*

"The gathering of Israel—the greatest cause on this earth—is *our* covenant responsibility. And this is *our* time! My invitation today is simple: share the gospel. Be you and hold up the light. Pray for heaven's help and follow spiritual promptings. Share your life normally and naturally; invite another person to come and see, to come and help, and to come and belong. And then rejoice as you and those you love receive the promised blessings."

### HOW DID GOD SHOW UP FOR YOU TODAY?

### WHAT CAN YOU ASK CHRIST TO HELP YOU CARRY RIGHT NOW?

### WHAT IS YOUR HOPE FOR TOMORROW?

DATE    /    /

## Scripture of the Day

*Micah 6:8*

"And what doth the Lord require of thee, but to do justly, and to love mercy, and to walk humbly with thy God?"

## Quote of the Day

*L. Todd Budge, "Giving Holiness to the Lord," October 2021*

"Something is made holy—whether it be our lives, our possessions, our time, or our talents—not simply by giving it up but rather by consecrating it to the Lord."

### HOW DID GOD SHOW UP FOR YOU TODAY?

### WHAT CAN YOU ASK CHRIST TO HELP YOU CARRY RIGHT NOW?

### WHAT IS YOUR HOPE FOR TOMORROW?

DATE    /    /

### Scripture of the Day

"I am the good shepherd: the good shepherd giveth his life for the sheep."

*John 10:11*

### Quote of the Day

"Never forget that you are a child of God, our Eternal Father, now and forever. He loves you, and the Church wants and needs you. Yes, we need you! We need your voices, talents, skills, goodness, and righteousness."

*M. Russell Ballard,
"Hope In Christ,"
April 2021*

## HOW DID GOD SHOW UP FOR YOU TODAY?

## WHAT CAN YOU ASK CHRIST TO HELP YOU CARRY RIGHT NOW?

## WHAT IS YOUR HOPE FOR TOMORROW?

DATE      /      /

## *Scripture of the Day*

"I say unto you, that there shall be no other name given nor any other way nor means whereby salvation can come unto the children of men, only in and through the name of Christ, the Lord Omnipotent."

*Mosiah 3:17*

## *Quote of the Day*

"As you make the continual strengthening of your testimony of Jesus Christ your highest priority, watch for miracles to happen in your life."

*Russell M. Nelson, "Overcome the World and Find Rest," October 2022*

### HOW DID GOD SHOW UP FOR YOU TODAY?

### WHAT CAN YOU ASK CHRIST TO HELP YOU CARRY RIGHT NOW?

### WHAT IS YOUR HOPE FOR TOMORROW?

DATE     /     /

## Scripture of the Day

*3 Nephi 17:5*

"And it came to pass that when Jesus had thus spoken, he cast his eyes round about again on the multitude, and beheld they were in tears, and did look steadfastly upon him as if they would ask him to tarry a little longer with them."

## Quote of the Day

*K. Brett Nattress, "Have I Truly Been Forgiven?" April 2023*

"The Savior had already spent a full day ministering to the people. Yet He had more to do—He was to visit His other sheep; He was to go to His Father. Notwithstanding these obligations, He discerned that the people desired for Him to tarry a little longer. Then, with the Savior's heart full of compassion, one of the greatest miracles in the history of the world occurred: He stayed. He blessed them. He ministered to their children one by one. He prayed for them; He wept with them. And He healed them. . . . His promise is eternal: He will heal us."

### HOW DID GOD SHOW UP FOR YOU TODAY?

### WHAT CAN YOU ASK CHRIST TO HELP YOU CARRY RIGHT NOW?

### WHAT IS YOUR HOPE FOR TOMORROW?

DATE ___ / ___ / ___

## Scripture of the Day

"He shall make intercession for all the children of men; and they that believe in him shall be saved."

*2 Nephi 2:9*

## Quote of the Day

"Learning, understanding, and living gospel principles strengthen our faith in the Savior, deepen our devotion to Him, and invite a multitude of blessings and spiritual gifts into our lives."

*David A. Bednar, "The Principles of My Gospel," April 2021*

### HOW DID GOD SHOW UP FOR YOU TODAY?

### WHAT CAN YOU ASK CHRIST TO HELP YOU CARRY RIGHT NOW?

### WHAT IS YOUR HOPE FOR TOMORROW?

DATE / /

## Scripture of the Day

*Doctrine and Covenants 25:10*

"And verily I say unto thee that thou shalt lay aside the things of this world, and seek for the things of a better."

## Quote of the Day

*Joy D. Jones, "An Especially Noble Calling," April 2020*

"Learning is integral to progression, especially as the constant companionship of the Holy Ghost teaches us what is needful for each of us to lay aside—meaning that which could *distract* us or *delay* our progression."

### HOW DID GOD SHOW UP FOR YOU TODAY?

### WHAT CAN YOU ASK CHRIST TO HELP YOU CARRY RIGHT NOW?

### WHAT IS YOUR HOPE FOR TOMORROW?

DATE      /      /

## Scripture of the Day

"Thou wilt shew me the path of life: in thy presence is fulness of joy; at thy right hand there are pleasures for evermore."

*Psalm 16:11*

## Quote of the Day

"The covenants God offers to His children do more than guide us. They bind us to Him, and, bound to Him, we can overcome all things."

*D. Todd Christofferson, "Why the Covenant Path," April 2021*

### HOW DID GOD SHOW UP FOR YOU TODAY?

### WHAT CAN YOU ASK CHRIST TO HELP YOU CARRY RIGHT NOW?

### WHAT IS YOUR HOPE FOR TOMORROW?

DATE      /      /

## Scripture of the Day

*1 John 3:2*

"Beloved, now are we the sons of God, and it doth not yet appear what we shall be: but we know that, when he shall appear, we shall be like him; for we shall see him as he is."

## Quote of the Day

*Dieter F. Uchtdorf, "God among Us," April 2021*

"If we earnestly keep practicing, always striving to keep God's commandments, and committing our efforts to repenting, enduring, and applying what we learn, line upon line, we will gather light into our souls. And though we may not fully comprehend our full potential now, 'we know that, when [the Savior] shall appear,' we will see His countenance in us and 'shall see him as he is.'"

### HOW DID GOD SHOW UP FOR YOU TODAY?

### WHAT CAN YOU ASK CHRIST TO HELP YOU CARRY RIGHT NOW?

### WHAT IS YOUR HOPE FOR TOMORROW?

DATE      /      /

## *Scripture of the Day*

*Moroni 7:16*

"For behold, the Spirit of Christ is given to every man, that he may know good from evil; wherefore, I show unto you the way to judge; for every thing which inviteth to do good, and to persuade to believe in Christ, is sent forth by the power and gift of Christ; wherefore ye may know with a perfect knowledge it is of God."

## *Quote of the Day*

Russell M. Nelson,
"Christ Is Risen;
Faith in Him Will
Move Mountains,"
April 2021

"Choose to believe in Jesus Christ. If you have doubts about God the Father and His Beloved Son or the validity of the Restoration or the veracity of Joseph Smith's divine calling as a prophet, *choose* to believe and stay faithful. Take your questions to the Lord and to other faithful sources. Study with the desire to believe rather than with the hope that you can find a flaw in the fabric of a prophet's life or a discrepancy in the scriptures. Stop increasing your doubts by rehearsing them with other doubters. Allow the Lord to lead you on your journey of spiritual discovery."

### HOW DID GOD SHOW UP FOR YOU TODAY?

### WHAT CAN YOU ASK CHRIST TO HELP YOU CARRY RIGHT NOW?

### WHAT IS YOUR HOPE FOR TOMORROW?

DATE        /        /

## Scripture of the Day

2 Nephi 31:20

"Wherefore, ye must press forward with a steadfastness in Christ, having a perfect brightness of hope, and a love of God and of all men. Wherefore, if ye shall press forward, feasting upon the word of Christ, and endure to the end, behold, thus saith the Father: Ye shall have eternal life."

## Quote of the Day

Kevin W. Pearson,
"Are You Still Willing?"
October 2022

"The covenant path is not a simple checklist; it is a process of spiritual growth and deepening commitment to the Lord Jesus Christ. The central purpose of every commandment, principle, covenant, and ordinance is to build faith and trust in Christ. Our determination to center our lives on Christ, therefore, must be consistent—not conditional, situational, or superficial."

### HOW DID GOD SHOW UP FOR YOU TODAY?

### WHAT CAN YOU ASK CHRIST TO HELP YOU CARRY RIGHT NOW?

### WHAT IS YOUR HOPE FOR TOMORROW?

DATE    /    /

## *Scripture of the Day*

*Doctrine and Covenants 6:33–34*

"Whatsoever ye sow, that shall ye also reap; therefore, if ye sow good ye shall also reap good for your reward. Therefore, fear not, little flock; do good; let earth and hell combine against you, for if ye are built upon my rock, they cannot prevail."

## *Quote of the Day*

*Dieter F. Uchtdorf, "God Will Do Something Unimaginable," October 2020*

"God will watch over and shepherd you during these times of uncertainty and fear. He knows you. He hears your pleas. He is faithful and dependable. He will fulfill His promises. . . . With Christ at the helm, things will not only be all right; they will be unimaginable."

### HOW DID GOD SHOW UP FOR YOU TODAY?

### WHAT CAN YOU ASK CHRIST TO HELP YOU CARRY RIGHT NOW?

### WHAT IS YOUR HOPE FOR TOMORROW?

DATE    /    /

## Scripture of the Day

*Doctrine and Covenants 122:7–8*

"And if thou shouldst be cast into the pit, or into the hands of murderers, and the sentence of death passed upon thee; if thou be cast into the deep; if the billowing surge conspire against thee; if fierce winds become thine enemy; if the heavens gather blackness, and all the elements combine to hedge up the way; and above all, if the very jaws of hell shall gape open the mouth wide after thee, know thou, my son, that all these things shall give thee experience, and shall be for thy good. The Son of Man hath descended below them all. Art thou greater than he?"

## Quote of the Day

*Russell M. Nelson, "The Answer Is Always Jesus Christ," April 2023*

"Whatever questions or problems you have, the answer is always found in the life and teachings of Jesus Christ. Learn more about His Atonement, His love, His mercy, His doctrine, and His restored gospel of healing and progression. Turn to Him! Follow Him!"

### HOW DID GOD SHOW UP FOR YOU TODAY?

### WHAT CAN YOU ASK CHRIST TO HELP YOU CARRY RIGHT NOW?

### WHAT IS YOUR HOPE FOR TOMORROW?

DATE    /    /

## *Scripture of the Day*

*Isaiah 12:2*

"Behold, God is my salvation; I will trust, and not be afraid: for the Lord Jehovah is my strength and my song; he also is become my salvation."

## *Quote of the Day*

*M. Russell Ballard, "Lovest Thou Me More Than These?" October 2021*

"Do the things of this world bring us the joy, happiness, and peace that the Savior offered to His disciples and that He offers to us? Only He can bring us true joy, happiness, and peace through our loving Him and following His teachings."

### HOW DID GOD SHOW UP FOR YOU TODAY?

### WHAT CAN YOU ASK CHRIST TO HELP YOU CARRY RIGHT NOW?

### WHAT IS YOUR HOPE FOR TOMORROW?

DATE    /    /

## Scripture of the Day

*Matthew 5:43–44*

"Ye have heard that it hath been said, Thou shalt love thy neighbour, and hate thine enemy. But I say unto you, Love your enemies, bless them that curse you, do good to them that hate you, and pray for them which despitefully use you, and persecute you."

## Quote of the Day

*Gerrit W. Gong, "Trust Again," October 2021*

"Whether we are coming home or going home, God is coming to meet us. In Him we can find faith and courage, wisdom and discernment to trust again. Likewise, He asks us to keep the light on for each other, to be more forgiving and less judgmental of ourselves and each other, so His Church can be a place where we feel at home, whether we are coming for the first time or returning."

### HOW DID GOD SHOW UP FOR YOU TODAY?

### WHAT CAN YOU ASK CHRIST TO HELP YOU CARRY RIGHT NOW?

### WHAT IS YOUR HOPE FOR TOMORROW?

DATE    /    /

## Scripture of the Day

*2 Nephi 31:10*

"And he said unto the children of men: Follow thou me. Wherefore, my beloved brethren, can we follow Jesus save we shall be willing to keep the commandments of the Father?"

## Quote of the Day

*Evan A. Schmutz, "Trusting the Doctrine of Christ," April 2023*

"If we *trust* the doctrine of Christ, we will trust Christ enough to live by His every word. We will make a lifelong study of Jesus Christ, His ministry, His teachings, and His infinite Atonement, including His glorious Resurrection. We will study His promises and the conditions upon which those promises are given. As we study, we will be filled with greater love for the Lord."

### HOW DID GOD SHOW UP FOR YOU TODAY?

### WHAT CAN YOU ASK CHRIST TO HELP YOU CARRY RIGHT NOW?

### WHAT IS YOUR HOPE FOR TOMORROW?

DATE      /      /

## Scripture of the Day

*Mosiah 2:17*

"And behold, I tell you these things that ye may learn wisdom; that ye may learn that when ye are in the service of your fellow beings ye are only in the service of your God."

## Quote of the Day

*Jeffrey R. Holland, "Lifted Up upon the Cross," October 2022*

"As we take up our crosses and follow Him, it would be tragic indeed if the weight of our challenges did not make us more empathetic for and more attentive to the burdens being carried by others."

### HOW DID GOD SHOW UP FOR YOU TODAY?

### WHAT CAN YOU ASK CHRIST TO HELP YOU CARRY RIGHT NOW?

### WHAT IS YOUR HOPE FOR TOMORROW?

DATE      /      /

## *Scripture of the Day*

*Jacob 5:66*

"For it grieveth me that I should lose the trees of my vineyard; wherefore ye shall clear away the bad according as the good shall grow, that the root and the top may be equal in strength, until the good shall overcome the bad, and the bad be hewn down and cast into the fire, that they cumber not the ground of my vineyard; and thus will I sweep away the bad out of my vineyard."

## *Quote of the Day*

*Sharon Eubank, "By Union of Feeling We Obtain Power with God," October 2020*

"Each of us is going to have deeply wounding experiences, things that should never happen. Each of us will also, at various times, allow pride and loftiness to corrupt the fruit we bear. But Jesus Christ is our Savior in all things. His power reaches to the very bottom and is reliably there for us when we call on Him. We all beg for mercy for our sins and failures. He freely gives it. And He asks us if we can give that same mercy and understanding to each other."

### HOW DID GOD SHOW UP FOR YOU TODAY?

### WHAT CAN YOU ASK CHRIST TO HELP YOU CARRY RIGHT NOW?

### WHAT IS YOUR HOPE FOR TOMORROW?

DATE          /          /

### Scripture of the Day

*Doctrine and Covenants 1:1*

"Hearken, O ye people of my church, saith the voice of him who dwells on high, and whose eyes are upon all men; yea, verily I say: Hearken ye people from afar; and ye that are upon the islands of the sea, listen together."

### Quote of the Day

*Russell M. Nelson, "Hear Him," April 2020*

"Our Father knows that when we are surrounded by uncertainty and fear, what will help us the very most is to hear His Son. Because when we seek to hear—truly hear—His Son, we will be guided to know what to do in any circumstance."

#### HOW DID GOD SHOW UP FOR YOU TODAY?

#### WHAT CAN YOU ASK CHRIST TO HELP YOU CARRY RIGHT NOW?

#### WHAT IS YOUR HOPE FOR TOMORROW?

DATE    /    /

### Scripture of the Day

"Cause me to hear thy lovingkindness in the morning; for in thee do I trust: cause me to know the way wherein I should walk; for I lift up my soul unto thee."

*Psalm 143:8*

### Quote of the Day

"My beloved friends, your Heavenly Father loves you with a perfect love. He has proven His love in endless ways, but above all by giving His Only Begotten Son as a sacrifice and as a gift to His children to make the return to our heavenly parents a reality."

*Dieter F. Uchtdorf, "God among Us," April 2021*

#### HOW DID GOD SHOW UP FOR YOU TODAY?

#### WHAT CAN YOU ASK CHRIST TO HELP YOU CARRY RIGHT NOW?

#### WHAT IS YOUR HOPE FOR TOMORROW?

DATE      /      /

## *Scripture of the Day*

*John 15:12*

"This is my commandment, That ye love one another, as I have loved you."

## *Quote of the Day*

*Jeffrey R. Holland, "The Greatest Possession," October 2021*

"When the love of God sets the tone for our own lives, for our relationships to each other and ultimately our feeling for all humankind, then old distinctions, limiting labels, and artificial divisions begin to pass away, and peace increases."

### HOW DID GOD SHOW UP FOR YOU TODAY?

### WHAT CAN YOU ASK CHRIST TO HELP YOU CARRY RIGHT NOW?

### WHAT IS YOUR HOPE FOR TOMORROW?

DATE ____ / ____ / ____

## Scripture of the Day

*Mosiah 16:8–9*

"There is a resurrection, therefore the grave hath no victory, and the sting of death is swallowed up in Christ. He is the light and the life of the world; yea, a light that is endless, that can never be darkened; yea, and also a life which is endless, that there can be no more death."

## Quote of the Day

*Russell M. Nelson, "Pure Truth, Pure Doctrine, and Pure Revelation," October 2021*

"This *is* The Church of Jesus Christ of Latter-day Saints. We are His covenant people. The Lord declared that He would hasten His work in its time, and He is doing so at an ever-increasing pace. We are privileged to participate in His holy work."

### HOW DID GOD SHOW UP FOR YOU TODAY?

### WHAT CAN YOU ASK CHRIST TO HELP YOU CARRY RIGHT NOW?

### WHAT IS YOUR HOPE FOR TOMORROW?

DATE    /    /

**Scripture of the Day**

1 Nephi 10:19

"For he that diligently seeketh shall find; and the mysteries of God shall be unfolded unto them, by the power of the Holy Ghost, as well in these times as in times of old, and as well in times of old as in times to come; wherefore, the course of the Lord is one eternal round."

**Quote of the Day**

Neil L. Andersen, "Drawing Closer to the Savior," October 2022

"We do our very best to protect our daily experiences so the influence of the Holy Ghost remains with us. We are a light to the world, and when necessary, we willingly choose to be different from others."

### HOW DID GOD SHOW UP FOR YOU TODAY?

### WHAT CAN YOU ASK CHRIST TO HELP YOU CARRY RIGHT NOW?

### WHAT IS YOUR HOPE FOR TOMORROW?

DATE    /    /

## Scripture of the Day

*Alma 42:14–15*

"And thus we see that all mankind were fallen, and they were in the grasp of justice; yea, the justice of God, which consigned them forever to be cut off from his presence. And now, the plan of mercy could not be brought about except an atonement should be made; therefore God himself atoneth for the sins of the world, to bring about the plan of mercy, to appease the demands of justice, that God might be a perfect, just God, and a merciful God also."

## Quote of the Day

*Gary E. Stevenson, "The Greatest Story Ever Told," April 2023*

"Studying regularly from [the Book of Mormon] about Jesus Christ will change your life. It will open your eyes to new possibilities. It will increase your hope and fill you with charity. Most of all, it will build and strengthen your faith in Jesus Christ and bless you with a sure knowledge that He and our Father know you, love you, and want you to find your way back home, with a capital *H*."

### HOW DID GOD SHOW UP FOR YOU TODAY?

### WHAT CAN YOU ASK CHRIST TO HELP YOU CARRY RIGHT NOW?

### WHAT IS YOUR HOPE FOR TOMORROW?

DATE      /      /

## *Scripture of the Day*

*Doctrine and Covenants 19:23*

"Learn of me, and listen to my words; walk in the meekness of my Spirit, and you shall have peace in me."

## *Quote of the Day*

*Russell M. Nelson, "Christ Is Risen; Faith in Him Will Move Mountains," April 2021*

"Become an engaged learner. Immerse yourself in the scriptures to understand better Christ's mission and ministry. Know the doctrine of Christ so that you understand its power for your life."

### HOW DID GOD SHOW UP FOR YOU TODAY?

### WHAT CAN YOU ASK CHRIST TO HELP YOU CARRY RIGHT NOW?

### WHAT IS YOUR HOPE FOR TOMORROW?

DATE        /        /

## Scripture of the Day

"Delight thyself also in the Lord; and he shall give thee the desires of thine heart. Commit thy way unto the Lord; trust also in him; and he shall bring it to pass."

*Psalm 37:4–5*

## Quote of the Day

"With Jesus Christ, the Master Healer and Savior, there can always be a new beginning; He always gives hope."

*Dieter F. Uchtdorf, "Jesus Christ Is the Strength of Parents," April 2023*

### HOW DID GOD SHOW UP FOR YOU TODAY?

### WHAT CAN YOU ASK CHRIST TO HELP YOU CARRY RIGHT NOW?

### WHAT IS YOUR HOPE FOR TOMORROW?

DATE     /     /

## Scripture of the Day

"Let us hold fast the profession of our faith without wavering; (for he is faithful that promised)."

*Hebrews 10:23*

## Quote of the Day

"You may feel small compared to the great sweep of what the Lord will do. If you do, I invite you to ask prayerfully how the Lord sees you. He knows you personally."

*Henry B. Eyring, "Bless in His Name," April 2021*

### HOW DID GOD SHOW UP FOR YOU TODAY?

### WHAT CAN YOU ASK CHRIST TO HELP YOU CARRY RIGHT NOW?

### WHAT IS YOUR HOPE FOR TOMORROW?

DATE      /      /

## Scripture of the Day

"The tender mercies of the Lord are over all those whom he hath chosen, because of their faith, to make them mighty even unto the power of deliverance."

*1 Nephi 1:20*

## Quote of the Day

*David A. Bednar, "The Tender Mercies of the Lord," April 2005*

"The simpleness, the sweetness, and the constancy of the tender mercies of the Lord will do much to fortify and protect us in the troubled times in which we do now and will yet live. When words cannot provide the solace we need or express the joy we feel, when it is simply futile to attempt to explain that which is unexplainable, when logic and reason cannot yield adequate understanding about the injustices and inequities of life, when mortal experience and evaluation are insufficient to produce a desired outcome, and when it seems that perhaps we are so totally alone, truly we are blessed by the tender mercies of the Lord and made mighty even unto the power of deliverance."

### HOW DID GOD SHOW UP FOR YOU TODAY?

### WHAT CAN YOU ASK CHRIST TO HELP YOU CARRY RIGHT NOW?

### WHAT IS YOUR HOPE FOR TOMORROW?

DATE      /      /

## Scripture of the Day

*2 Nephi 2:26*

"And the Messiah cometh in the fulness of time, that he may redeem the children of men from the fall. And because that they are redeemed from the fall they have become free forever, knowing good from evil; to act for themselves and not to be acted upon, save it be by the punishment of the law at the great and last day, according to the commandments which God hath given."

## Quote of the Day

*Russell M. Nelson, "Joy and Spiritual Survival," October 2016*

"Joy comes from and because of [Jesus Christ]. He is the source of all joy. . . . For Latter-day Saints, Jesus Christ is joy!"

### HOW DID GOD SHOW UP FOR YOU TODAY?

### WHAT CAN YOU ASK CHRIST TO HELP YOU CARRY RIGHT NOW?

### WHAT IS YOUR HOPE FOR TOMORROW?

DATE     /     /

## Scripture of the Day

"And he shall go forth, suffering pains and afflictions and temptations of every kind; and this that the word might be fulfilled which saith he will take upon him the pains and the sicknesses of his people."

*Alma 7:11*

## Quote of the Day

"Whether they are personal struggles, family troubles, or community crises, peace will come as we trust that God's Only Begotten Son has power to soothe our aching souls."

*Jean B. Bingham, "That Your Joy Might Be Full," October 2017*

### HOW DID GOD SHOW UP FOR YOU TODAY?

### WHAT CAN YOU ASK CHRIST TO HELP YOU CARRY RIGHT NOW?

### WHAT IS YOUR HOPE FOR TOMORROW?

DATE    /    /

## *Scripture of the Day*

*Doctrine and Covenants 121:28*

"A time to come in the which nothing shall be withheld, whether there be one God or many gods, they shall be manifest."

## *Quote of the Day*

*Jeffrey R. Holland, "Waiting on the Lord," October 2020*

"Christianity is comforting, but it is often not comfortable. The path to holiness and happiness here and hereafter is a long and sometimes rocky one. It takes time and tenacity to walk it. But, of course, the reward for doing so is monumental."

### HOW DID GOD SHOW UP FOR YOU TODAY?

### WHAT CAN YOU ASK CHRIST TO HELP YOU CARRY RIGHT NOW?

### WHAT IS YOUR HOPE FOR TOMORROW?

DATE    /    /

## Scripture of the Day

"I have set the Lord always before me: because he is at my right hand, I shall not be moved. Therefore my heart is glad, and my glory rejoiceth: my flesh also shall rest in hope."

*Psalm 16:8–9*

## Quote of the Day

"There is reason for optimism: it is that the Light of Christ is placed in every newborn child. With that universal gift comes a sense of what is right, a desire to love and be loved. There is an inborn sense of justice and truth in every child of God as he or she comes into mortality."

*Henry B. Eyring, "Finding Personal Peace," April 2023*

### HOW DID GOD SHOW UP FOR YOU TODAY?

### WHAT CAN YOU ASK CHRIST TO HELP YOU CARRY RIGHT NOW?

### WHAT IS YOUR HOPE FOR TOMORROW?

DATE      /      /

## Scripture of the Day

*John 16:33*

"These things I have spoken unto you, that in me ye might have peace. In the world ye shall have tribulation: but be of good cheer; I have overcome the world."

## Quote of the Day

*Dieter F. Uchtdorf, "God among Us," April 2021*

"Because of Jesus Christ, our failures do not have to define us. They can refine us. Like a musician rehearsing scales, we can see our missteps, flaws, and sins as opportunities for greater self-awareness, deeper and more honest love for others, and refinement through repentance. If we repent, mistakes do not disqualify us. They are part of our progress."

### HOW DID GOD SHOW UP FOR YOU TODAY?

### WHAT CAN YOU ASK CHRIST TO HELP YOU CARRY RIGHT NOW?

### WHAT IS YOUR HOPE FOR TOMORROW?

DATE    /    /

## Scripture of the Day

*3 Nephi 11:15–17*

"And it came to pass that the multitude went forth, and thrust their hands into his side, and did feel the prints of the nails in his hands and in his feet; and this they did do, going forth one by one until they had all gone forth, and did see with their eyes and did feel with their hands, and did know of a surety and did bear record, that it was he, of whom it was written by the prophets, that should come. And when they had all gone forth and had witnessed for themselves, they did cry out with one accord, saying: Hosanna! Blessed be the name of the Most High God! And they did fall down at the feet of Jesus, and did worship him."

## Quote of the Day

*Gary E. Stevenson, "The Greatest Story Ever Told," April 2023*

"We cannot *stand* as witnesses of Jesus Christ until we can *bear* witness of Him. The Book of Mormon is another witness of Jesus Christ because throughout its sacred pages, one prophet after another testifies not only that Christ would come but that He *did* come. . . . Anytime we read and study from the Book of Mormon, we can expect remarkable outcomes."

### HOW DID GOD SHOW UP FOR YOU TODAY?

### WHAT CAN YOU ASK CHRIST TO HELP YOU CARRY RIGHT NOW?

### WHAT IS YOUR HOPE FOR TOMORROW?

DATE      /      /

## *Scripture of the Day*

*2 Nephi 9:52*

"Remember the words of your God; pray unto him continually by day, and give thanks unto his holy name by night. Let your hearts rejoice."

## *Quote of the Day*

*José A. Teixeira, "Remember Your Way Back Home," April 2021*

"God is fully aware of each one of us and ready to listen to our prayers. When we remember to pray, we find His sustaining love, and the more we pray to our Father in Heaven in Christ's name, the more we bring the Savior into our life and the better we will recognize the path He has marked to our heavenly home."

### HOW DID GOD SHOW UP FOR YOU TODAY?

### WHAT CAN YOU ASK CHRIST TO HELP YOU CARRY RIGHT NOW?

### WHAT IS YOUR HOPE FOR TOMORROW?

DATE ____ / ____ / ____

## Scripture of the Day

*3 Nephi 11:29*

"For verily, verily I say unto you, he that hath the spirit of contention is not of me, but is of the devil, who is the father of contention, and he stirreth up the hearts of men to contend with anger, one with another."

## Quote of the Day

*Russell M. Nelson, "Peacemakers Needed," April 2023*

"The Savior's Atonement made it possible for us to overcome *all* evil—including contention. Make no mistake about it: contention *is* evil! Jesus Christ declared that those who have 'the spirit of contention' are not of Him but are 'of the devil, who is the father of contention, and [the devil] stirreth up the hearts of men to contend with anger, one with another.' Those who foster contention are taking a page out of Satan's playbook, whether they realize it or not. 'No man can serve two masters.' We cannot support Satan with our verbal assaults and then think that we can still serve God."

### HOW DID GOD SHOW UP FOR YOU TODAY?

### WHAT CAN YOU ASK CHRIST TO HELP YOU CARRY RIGHT NOW?

### WHAT IS YOUR HOPE FOR TOMORROW?

DATE    /    /

## Scripture of the Day

*Deuteronomy 31:8*

"And the Lord, he it is that doth go before thee; he will be with thee, he will not fail thee, neither forsake thee: fear not, neither be dismayed."

## Quote of the Day

*M. Russell Ballard, "Missionary Service Blessed My Life Forever," April 2022*

"The Lord knows you."

### HOW DID GOD SHOW UP FOR YOU TODAY?

### WHAT CAN YOU ASK CHRIST TO HELP YOU CARRY RIGHT NOW?

### WHAT IS YOUR HOPE FOR TOMORROW?

DATE    /    /

## *Scripture of the Day*

*Matthew 6:6*

"But thou, when thou prayest, enter into thy closet, and when thou hast shut thy door, pray to thy Father which is in secret; and thy Father which seeth in secret shall reward thee openly."

## **Quote of the Day**

*Ronald A. Rasband, "Behold! I Am a God of Miracles," April 2021*

"Miracles can come as answers to prayer. They are not always what we ask for or what we expect, but when we trust in the Lord, He will be there, and He will be right. He will suit the miracle to the moment we need it."

### HOW DID GOD SHOW UP FOR YOU TODAY?

### WHAT CAN YOU ASK CHRIST TO HELP YOU CARRY RIGHT NOW?

### WHAT IS YOUR HOPE FOR TOMORROW?

DATE     /     /

## Scripture of the Day

*Alma 42:15*

"And now, the plan of mercy could not be brought about except an atonement should be made; therefore God himself atoneth for the sins of the world, to bring about the plan of mercy, to appease the demands of justice, that God might be a perfect, just God, and a merciful God also."

## Quote of the Day

*Gerrit W. Gong, "Hosanna and Hallelujah—The Living Jesus Christ: The Heart of Restoration and Easter," April 2020*

"Because 'God himself atoneth for the sins of the world,' the Lord's Atonement can make whole not only what was but also what can be. Because He knows our pains, afflictions, sicknesses, our 'temptations of every kind,' He can, with mercy, succor us according to our infirmities. Because God is 'a perfect, just God, and a merciful God also,' the plan of mercy can 'appease the demands of justice.' We repent and do all we can. He encircles us eternally 'in the arms of his love.'"

### HOW DID GOD SHOW UP FOR YOU TODAY?

### WHAT CAN YOU ASK CHRIST TO HELP YOU CARRY RIGHT NOW?

### WHAT IS YOUR HOPE FOR TOMORROW?

DATE    /    /

## Scripture of the Day

"And thus we see that by small means the Lord can bring about great things."

*1 Nephi 16:29*

## Quote of the Day

"'Give,' said the little stream, / As it hurried down the hill; / 'I'm small, I know, but wherever I go / The fields grow greener still.' Yes, each of us is small, but together, as we hasten to give to God and our fellow men, wherever we go lives are enriched and blessed."

*L. Todd Budge, "Giving Holiness to the Lord," October 2021*

### HOW DID GOD SHOW UP FOR YOU TODAY?

### WHAT CAN YOU ASK CHRIST TO HELP YOU CARRY RIGHT NOW?

### WHAT IS YOUR HOPE FOR TOMORROW?

DATE      /      /

## *Scripture of the Day*

*Mosiah 3:19*

"For the natural man is an enemy to God, and has been from the fall of Adam, and will be, forever and ever, unless he yields to the enticings of the Holy Spirit, and putteth off the natural man and becometh a saint through the atonement of Christ the Lord, and becometh as a child, submissive, meek, humble, patient, full of love, willing to submit to all things which the Lord seeth fit to inflict upon him, even as a child doth submit to his father."

## *Quote of the Day*

*Russell M. Nelson,
"Let God Prevail,"
October 2020*

"When your greatest desire is to let God prevail, to be part of Israel, so many decisions become easier. So many issues become nonissues! . . . It takes both faith and courage to let God prevail. It takes persistent, rigorous spiritual work to repent and to put off the natural man through the Atonement of Jesus Christ. It takes consistent, daily effort to develop personal habits to study the gospel, to learn more about Heavenly Father and Jesus Christ, and to seek and respond to personal revelation."

### HOW DID GOD SHOW UP FOR YOU TODAY?

### WHAT CAN YOU ASK CHRIST TO HELP YOU CARRY RIGHT NOW?

### WHAT IS YOUR HOPE FOR TOMORROW?

DATE      /      /

## Scripture of the Day

*Psalm 46:5*

"God is in the midst of her; she shall not be moved: God shall help her, and that right early."

## Quote of the Day

*Neil L. Andersen, "Drawing Closer to the Savior," October 2022*

"We realize that as evil increases in the world, our spiritual survival, and the spiritual survival of those we love, will require that we more fully nurture, fortify, and strengthen the roots of our faith in Jesus Christ. The Apostle Paul counseled us to be rooted, grounded, and settled in our love for the Savior and our determination to follow Him. Today and the days ahead require more focused and concentrated effort, guarding against diversions and carelessness."

### HOW DID GOD SHOW UP FOR YOU TODAY?

### WHAT CAN YOU ASK CHRIST TO HELP YOU CARRY RIGHT NOW?

### WHAT IS YOUR HOPE FOR TOMORROW?

DATE     /     /

### Scripture of the Day

"And he saith unto them, Follow me, and I will make you fishers of men. And they straightway left their nets, and followed him."

*Matthew 4:19–20*

### Quote of the Day

"Being a disciple of Jesus Christ involves more than just hoping or believing. It calls for effort, movement, and commitment. It requires that we do something, being 'doers of the word, and not hearers only.'"

*Rebecca L. Craven, "Do What Mattereth Most," April 2022*

#### HOW DID GOD SHOW UP FOR YOU TODAY?

#### WHAT CAN YOU ASK CHRIST TO HELP YOU CARRY RIGHT NOW?

#### WHAT IS YOUR HOPE FOR TOMORROW?

DATE      /      /

## Scripture of the Day

*2 Nephi 26:30*

"Wherefore, the Lord God hath given a commandment that all men should have charity, which charity is love. And except they should have charity they were nothing. Wherefore, if they should have charity they would not suffer the laborer in Zion to perish."

## Quote of the Day

*Ulisses Soares, "Followers of the Prince of Peace," April 2023*

"When we think of charity, our minds usually turn to generous acts and donations to relieve the suffering of those who are experiencing physical, material, or emotional difficulties. Still, charity is not only related to something we donate to someone, but it's an attribute of the Savior and can become part of our character. It is not surprising that the Lord instructed us to clothe ourselves 'with the bond of charity, . . . which is the bond of perfectness and peace.' Without charity, we are nothing and we cannot inherit the place the Lord has prepared for us in the mansions of our Heavenly Father."

### HOW DID GOD SHOW UP FOR YOU TODAY?

### WHAT CAN YOU ASK CHRIST TO HELP YOU CARRY RIGHT NOW?

### WHAT IS YOUR HOPE FOR TOMORROW?

DATE    /    /

## Scripture of the Day

*1 Nephi 14:14*

"And it came to pass that I, Nephi, beheld the power of the Lamb of God, that it descended upon the saints of the church of the Lamb, and upon the covenant people of the Lord, who were scattered upon all the face of the earth; and they were armed with righteousness and with the power of God in great glory."

## Quote of the Day

*Russell M. Nelson, "Hear Him," April 2020*

"*You*, my brothers and sisters, are among those men, women, and children whom Nephi saw. Think of that! Regardless of where you live or what your circumstances are, the Lord Jesus Christ is *your* Savior."

### HOW DID GOD SHOW UP FOR YOU TODAY?

### WHAT CAN YOU ASK CHRIST TO HELP YOU CARRY RIGHT NOW?

### WHAT IS YOUR HOPE FOR TOMORROW?

DATE     /     /

## *Scripture of the Day*

*1 Nephi 21:14–16*

"But, behold, Zion hath said: The Lord hath forsaken me, and my Lord hath forgotten me—but he will show that he hath not . . . yet will I not forget thee, O house of Israel. Behold, I have graven thee upon the palms of my hands."

## *Quote of the Day*

*David A. Bednar, "With the Power of God in Great Glory," October 2021*

"We take the Savior's yoke upon us as we learn about, worthily receive, and honor sacred covenants and ordinances. We are bound securely to and with the Savior as we faithfully remember and do our best to live in accordance with the obligations we have accepted. And that bond with Him is the source of spiritual strength in every season of our lives."

### HOW DID GOD SHOW UP FOR YOU TODAY?

### WHAT CAN YOU ASK CHRIST TO HELP YOU CARRY RIGHT NOW?

### WHAT IS YOUR HOPE FOR TOMORROW?

DATE   /   /

## Scripture of the Day

*Psalm 18:1–2*

"I will love thee, O Lord, my strength. The Lord is my rock, and my fortress, and my deliverer; my God, my strength, in whom I will trust."

## Quote of the Day

*Neil L. Andersen, "My Mind Caught Hold upon This Thought of Jesus Christ," April 2023*

"Filling our mind with the power of Jesus Christ does not mean that He is the only thought we have. But it does mean that all our thoughts are circumscribed in His love, His life and teachings, and His atoning sacrifice and glorious Resurrection."

### HOW DID GOD SHOW UP FOR YOU TODAY?

### WHAT CAN YOU ASK CHRIST TO HELP YOU CARRY RIGHT NOW?

### WHAT IS YOUR HOPE FOR TOMORROW?

DATE    /    /

## Scripture of the Day
*Romans 8:16–17*

"The Spirit itself beareth witness with our spirit, that we are the children of God: And if children, then heirs; heirs of God, and joint-heirs with Christ if so be that we suffer with him, that we may be also glorified together."

## Quote of the Day
*Dieter F. Uchtdorf, "God among Us," April 2021*

"It is astonishing what we can learn when we look a little closer at our Heavenly Father's plan of salvation and exaltation, the plan of happiness, for His children. When we feel insignificant, cast off, and forgotten, we learn that we may be assured that God has not forgotten us—in fact, that He offers to all His children something unimaginable: to become 'heirs of God, and joint-heirs with Christ.'"

### HOW DID GOD SHOW UP FOR YOU TODAY?

### WHAT CAN YOU ASK CHRIST TO HELP YOU CARRY RIGHT NOW?

### WHAT IS YOUR HOPE FOR TOMORROW?

DATE    /    /

## Scripture of the Day

"And I was led by the Spirit, not knowing beforehand the things which I should do."

*1 Nephi 4:6*

## Quote of the Day

"Revelation comes to us in proportion to the degree to which we have sought to take the doctrine of Christ into our hearts and implement it in our lives."

*Henry B. Eyring, "The Faith to Ask and Then to Act," October 2021*

### HOW DID GOD SHOW UP FOR YOU TODAY?

### WHAT CAN YOU ASK CHRIST TO HELP YOU CARRY RIGHT NOW?

### WHAT IS YOUR HOPE FOR TOMORROW?

DATE       /       /

## *Scripture of the Day*

"I say unto you, that there shall be no other name given nor any other way nor means whereby salvation can come unto the children of men, only in and through the name of Christ, the Lord Omnipotent."

*Mosiah 3:17*

## *Quote of the Day*

"As you make the continual strengthening of your testimony of Jesus Christ your highest priority, watch for miracles to happen in your life."

*Russell M. Nelson, "Overcome the World and Find Rest," October 2022*

### HOW DID GOD SHOW UP FOR YOU TODAY?

### WHAT CAN YOU ASK CHRIST TO HELP YOU CARRY RIGHT NOW?

### WHAT IS YOUR HOPE FOR TOMORROW?

DATE    /    /

## Scripture of the Day

*Moroni 7:48*

"Wherefore, my beloved brethren, pray unto the Father with all the energy of heart, that ye may be filled with this love, which he hath bestowed upon all who are true followers of his Son, Jesus Christ; that ye may become the sons of God; that when he shall appear we shall be like him, for we shall see him as he is; that we may have this hope; that we may be purified even as he is pure."

## Quote of the Day

*Michelle D. Craig, "Eyes to See," October 2020*

"As with all gifts the Father so willingly offers, seeing deeply requires us to ask *Him*—and then *act*. Ask to see others as He does—as His true sons and daughters with infinite and divine potential. Then *act* by loving, serving, and affirming their worth and potential as prompted. As this becomes the pattern of our lives, we will find ourselves becoming 'true followers of . . . Jesus Christ.' Others will be able to trust our hearts with theirs. And in this pattern we will also discover *our own* true identity and purpose."

### HOW DID GOD SHOW UP FOR YOU TODAY?

### WHAT CAN YOU ASK CHRIST TO HELP YOU CARRY RIGHT NOW?

### WHAT IS YOUR HOPE FOR TOMORROW?

DATE / /

## *Scripture of the Day*

"He telleth the number of the stars; he calleth them all by their names. Great is our Lord, and of great power: his understanding is infinite."

*Psalm 147:4–5*

## *Quote of the Day*

"What would you do if you had more faith? Think about it. Write about it. Then *receive more* faith by doing something that *requires* more faith."

*Russell M. Nelson, "Christ Is Risen; Faith in Him Will Move Mountains," April 2021*

### HOW DID GOD SHOW UP FOR YOU TODAY?

### WHAT CAN YOU ASK CHRIST TO HELP YOU CARRY RIGHT NOW?

### WHAT IS YOUR HOPE FOR TOMORROW?

DATE     /     /

## Scripture of the Day

*John 4:35*

"Say not ye, There are yet four months, and then cometh harvest? behold, I say unto you, Lift up your eyes, and look on the fields; for they are white already to harvest."

## Quote of the Day

*Mark A. Bragg,*
*"Christlike Poise,"*
*April 2023*

"Poise comes when we see things from an eternal perspective. The Lord has counseled His disciples to 'lift up your eyes' and to 'let the solemnities of eternity rest upon your minds.' By framing challenging times within an eternal plan, pressure becomes a privilege to love, serve, teach, and bless. An eternal view enables Christlike poise."

### HOW DID GOD SHOW UP FOR YOU TODAY?

### WHAT CAN YOU ASK CHRIST TO HELP YOU CARRY RIGHT NOW?

### WHAT IS YOUR HOPE FOR TOMORROW?

DATE       /       /

## Scripture of the Day

"And I, Nephi, did go into the mount oft, and I did pray oft unto the Lord; wherefore the Lord showed unto me great things."

*1 Nephi 18:3*

## Quote of the Day

"We all have things, large and small, we need to sacrifice in order to follow Jesus Christ more completely. Our sacrifices show what we truly value. Sacrifices are sacred and honored by the Lord."

*Dieter F. Uchtdorf, "Our Heartfelt All," April 2022*

### HOW DID GOD SHOW UP FOR YOU TODAY?

### WHAT CAN YOU ASK CHRIST TO HELP YOU CARRY RIGHT NOW?

### WHAT IS YOUR HOPE FOR TOMORROW?

DATE     /     /

## Scripture of the Day

*2 Nephi 33:6*

"I glory in plainness; I glory in truth; I glory in my Jesus."

## Quote of the Day

*Russell M. Nelson, "Joy and Spiritual Survival," October 2016*

"The joy we feel has little to do with the circumstances of our lives and everything to do with the focus of our lives. When the focus of our lives is on God's plan of salvation . . . and Jesus Christ and His gospel, we can feel joy regardless of what is happening—or not happening—in our lives."

### HOW DID GOD SHOW UP FOR YOU TODAY?

### WHAT CAN YOU ASK CHRIST TO HELP YOU CARRY RIGHT NOW?

### WHAT IS YOUR HOPE FOR TOMORROW?

DATE    /    /

## Scripture of the Day

*Ether 3:14*

"Behold, I am he who was prepared from the foundation of the world to redeem my people. Behold, I am Jesus Christ. I am the Father and the Son. In me shall all mankind have life, and that eternally, even they who shall believe on my name; and they shall become my sons and my daughters."

## Quote of the Day

*Lisa L. Harkness, "Peace, Be Still," October 2020*

"Regardless of our circumstances, we can intentionally make efforts to build and increase our faith in Jesus Christ. It is strengthened when we remember that we are children of God and that He loves us. Our faith grows as we experiment on the word of God with hope and diligence, trying our very best to follow Christ's teachings. Our faith increases as we choose to believe rather than doubt, forgive rather than judge, repent rather than rebel. Our faith is refined as we patiently rely on the merits and mercy and grace of the Holy Messiah."

### HOW DID GOD SHOW UP FOR YOU TODAY?

### WHAT CAN YOU ASK CHRIST TO HELP YOU CARRY RIGHT NOW?

### WHAT IS YOUR HOPE FOR TOMORROW?

DATE        /        /

## Scripture of the Day

*Psalm 40:16*

"Let all those that seek thee rejoice and be glad in thee: let such as love thy salvation say continually, The Lord be magnified."

## Quote of the Day

*Russell M. Nelson, "Christ Is Risen; Faith in Him Will Move Mountains," April 2021*

"Internalize the truth that the Atonement of Jesus Christ applies to you. He took upon Himself your misery, your mistakes, your weakness, and your sins. He paid the compensatory price and provided the power for you to move every mountain you will ever face. You obtain that power with your faith, trust, and willingness to follow Him."

### HOW DID GOD SHOW UP FOR YOU TODAY?

### WHAT CAN YOU ASK CHRIST TO HELP YOU CARRY RIGHT NOW?

### WHAT IS YOUR HOPE FOR TOMORROW?

DATE     /     /

## *Scripture of the Day*

"But straightway Jesus spake unto them, saying, Be of good cheer; it is I; be not afraid."

*Matthew 14:27*

## *Quote of the Day*

"'Be of good cheer' is the commandment from the Lord, not be of good fear."

*Jeremy R. Jaggi, "Let Patience Have Her Perfect Work, and Count It All Joy!" October 2020*

### HOW DID GOD SHOW UP FOR YOU TODAY?

### WHAT CAN YOU ASK CHRIST TO HELP YOU CARRY RIGHT NOW?

### WHAT IS YOUR HOPE FOR TOMORROW?

DATE      /      /

## *Scripture of the Day*

*Mosiah 24:14*

"And I will also ease the burdens which are put upon your shoulders, that even you cannot feel them upon your backs, even while you are in bondage; and this will I do that ye may stand as witness for me hereafter, and that ye may know of a surety that I, the Lord God, do visit my people in their afflictions."

## *Quote of the Day*

*Russell M. Nelson, "Christ Is Risen; Faith in Him Will Move Mountains," April 2021*

"Your growing faith in Him will move mountains—not the mountains of rock that beautify the earth but the mountains of misery in your lives. Your flourishing faith will help you turn challenges into unparalleled growth and opportunity."

### HOW DID GOD SHOW UP FOR YOU TODAY?

### WHAT CAN YOU ASK CHRIST TO HELP YOU CARRY RIGHT NOW?

### WHAT IS YOUR HOPE FOR TOMORROW?

DATE      /      /

## Scripture of the Day

*Alma 5:26*

"If ye have experienced a change of heart, and if ye have felt to sing the song of redeeming love, I would ask, can ye feel so now?"

## Quote of the Day

*Susan H. Porter, "God's Love: The Most Joyous to the Soul," October 2021*

"When you know and understand how completely you are loved as a child of God, it changes everything. It changes the way you feel about yourself when you make mistakes. It changes how you feel when difficult things happen. It changes your view of God's commandments. It changes your view of others and of your capacity to make a difference."

### HOW DID GOD SHOW UP FOR YOU TODAY?

### WHAT CAN YOU ASK CHRIST TO HELP YOU CARRY RIGHT NOW?

### WHAT IS YOUR HOPE FOR TOMORROW?

DATE    /    /

**Scripture of the Day**

1 Nephi 9:6

"But the Lord knoweth all things from the beginning; wherefore, he prepareth a way to accomplish all his works among the children of men; for behold, he hath all power unto the fulfilling of all his words."

**Quote of the Day**

Gerrit W. Gong,
"Trust Again,"
October 2021

"Trust becomes real when we do hard things with faith. Service and sacrifice increase capacity and refine hearts. Trust in God and each other brings heaven's blessings."

## HOW DID GOD SHOW UP FOR YOU TODAY?

## WHAT CAN YOU ASK CHRIST TO HELP YOU CARRY RIGHT NOW?

## WHAT IS YOUR HOPE FOR TOMORROW?

DATE    /    /

## Scripture of the Day

"For he shall give his angels charge over thee, to keep thee in all thy ways."

*Psalm 91:11*

## Quote of the Day

"Our Heavenly Father and His Beloved Son, Jesus Christ, stand ready to help you. I urge you to increase your efforts to seek Their help."

*Russell M. Nelson, "Focus on the Temple," October 2022*

### HOW DID GOD SHOW UP FOR YOU TODAY?

### WHAT CAN YOU ASK CHRIST TO HELP YOU CARRY RIGHT NOW?

### WHAT IS YOUR HOPE FOR TOMORROW?

DATE  /  /

## Scripture of the Day

"I can do all things through Christ which strengtheneth me."

*Philippians 4:13*

## Quote of the Day

"You can build a joyful, happy life because Jesus Christ is your strength. You can find confidence, peace, safety, happiness, and belonging now and eternally, because you will find all of it in Jesus Christ, in His gospel, and in His Church."

*Dieter F. Uchtdorf, "Jesus Christ Is the Strength of Youth," October 2022*

### HOW DID GOD SHOW UP FOR YOU TODAY?

### WHAT CAN YOU ASK CHRIST TO HELP YOU CARRY RIGHT NOW?

### WHAT IS YOUR HOPE FOR TOMORROW?

DATE      /      /

## Scripture of the Day

*Psalm 34:14*

"Depart from evil, and do good; seek peace, and pursue it."

## Quote of the Day

*Jeffrey R. Holland,
"The Ministry of
Reconciliation,"
October 2018*

"Friends, in our shared ministry of reconciliation, I ask us to be peacemakers—to love peace, to seek peace, to create peace, to cherish peace. I make that appeal in the name of the Prince of Peace, who knows everything about being 'wounded in the house of [His] friends' but who still found the strength to forgive and forget—and to heal—and be happy."

### HOW DID GOD SHOW UP FOR YOU TODAY?

### WHAT CAN YOU ASK CHRIST TO HELP YOU CARRY RIGHT NOW?

### WHAT IS YOUR HOPE FOR TOMORROW?

DATE    /    /

## Scripture of the Day

"Teach them to never be weary of good works, but to be meek and lowly in heart; for such shall find rest to their souls."

*Alma 37:34*

## Quote of the Day

"The Church of Jesus Christ is under divine mandate to care for the poor. It is one of the pillars of the work of salvation and exaltation."

*Sharon Eubank, "I Pray He'll Use Us," October 2021*

### HOW DID GOD SHOW UP FOR YOU TODAY?

### WHAT CAN YOU ASK CHRIST TO HELP YOU CARRY RIGHT NOW?

### WHAT IS YOUR HOPE FOR TOMORROW?

DATE       /       /

**Scripture of the Day**

---

Romans 8:28

"And we know that all things work together for good to them that love God, to them who are the called according to his purpose."

**Quote of the Day**

---

Henry B. Eyring, "Steady in the Storms," April 2022

"When the storms in life come, you can be steady because you are standing on the rock of your faith in Jesus Christ. That faith will lead you to daily repentance and consistent covenant keeping. Then you will always remember Him. And through the storms of hatred and wickedness, you will feel steady and hopeful. More than that, you will find yourself reaching out to lift others to safety on the rock with you. Faith in Jesus Christ always leads to greater hope and to feelings of charity toward others, which is the true love of Christ."

### HOW DID GOD SHOW UP FOR YOU TODAY?

### WHAT CAN YOU ASK CHRIST TO HELP YOU CARRY RIGHT NOW?

### WHAT IS YOUR HOPE FOR TOMORROW?

DATE    /    /

## Scripture of the Day

*Alma 4:15*

"Nevertheless the Spirit of the Lord did not fail him."

## Quote of the Day

*Gerrit W. Gong, "Trust Again," October 2021*

"We can always trust God. The Lord knows us better and loves us more than we know or love ourselves. His infinite love and perfect knowledge of past, present, and future make His covenants and promises constant and sure."

### HOW DID GOD SHOW UP FOR YOU TODAY?

### WHAT CAN YOU ASK CHRIST TO HELP YOU CARRY RIGHT NOW?

### WHAT IS YOUR HOPE FOR TOMORROW?

DATE      /      /

## Scripture of the Day

*3 Nephi 27:27*

"And know ye that ye shall be judges of this people, according to the judgment which I shall give unto you, which shall be just. Therefore, what manner of men ought ye to be? Verily I say unto you, even as I am."

## Quote of the Day

*Scott D. Whiting, "Becoming like Him," October 2020*

"What if becoming 'even as [He is]' is not figurative, even in our mortal condition? What if it is, to some degree, attainable in this life and, indeed, a prerequisite to being with Him again? What if 'even as I am' is exactly and precisely what is meant by the Savior? Then what? What level of effort would we be willing to give to invite His miraculous power into our lives so that we can change our very nature?"

### HOW DID GOD SHOW UP FOR YOU TODAY?

### WHAT CAN YOU ASK CHRIST TO HELP YOU CARRY RIGHT NOW?

### WHAT IS YOUR HOPE FOR TOMORROW?

DATE    /    /

## Scripture of the Day

"For with what judgment ye judge, ye shall be judged: and with what measure ye mete, it shall be measured to you again."

*Matthew 7:2*

## Quote of the Day

"If a couple in your ward gets divorced, or a young missionary returns home early, or a teenager doubts his testimony, they do not need your judgment. They need to experience the pure love of Jesus Christ reflected in your words and actions. If a friend on social media has strong political or social views that violate everything you believe in, an angry, cutting retort by you will not help. Building bridges of understanding will require much more of you, but that is exactly what your friend needs."

*Russell M. Nelson, "Peacemakers Needed," April 2023*

### HOW DID GOD SHOW UP FOR YOU TODAY?

### WHAT CAN YOU ASK CHRIST TO HELP YOU CARRY RIGHT NOW?

### WHAT IS YOUR HOPE FOR TOMORROW?

DATE      /      /

**Scripture of the Day**

"The Lord also will be a refuge for the oppressed, a refuge in times of trouble."

*Psalm 9:9*

**Quote of the Day**

"As we face the storms of life, I know that if we make our best effort and rely upon Jesus Christ and His Atonement as our refuge, we will be blessed with the relief, comfort, strength, temperance, and peace that we are seeking, with certainty in our hearts."

*Ricardo P. Giménez, "Finding Refuge from the Storms of Life," April 2020*

### HOW DID GOD SHOW UP FOR YOU TODAY?

### WHAT CAN YOU ASK CHRIST TO HELP YOU CARRY RIGHT NOW?

### WHAT IS YOUR HOPE FOR TOMORROW?

DATE         /         /

**Scripture of the Day**

Alma 32:27

"But behold, if ye will awake and arouse your faculties, even to an experiment upon my words, and exercise a particle of faith, yea, even if ye can no more than desire to believe, let this desire work in you, even until ye believe in a manner that ye can give place for a portion of my words."

**Quote of the Day**

S. Mark Palmer, "Our Sorrow Shall Be Turned into Joy," April 2021

"I invite all who feel sorrow, all who wrestle with doubt, all who wonder what happens after we die, to place your faith in Christ. I promise that if you desire to believe, then *act* in faith and *follow* the whisperings of the Spirit, you will find joy in this life and in the world to come."

### HOW DID GOD SHOW UP FOR YOU TODAY?

### WHAT CAN YOU ASK CHRIST TO HELP YOU CARRY RIGHT NOW?

### WHAT IS YOUR HOPE FOR TOMORROW?

DATE      /      /

**Scripture of the Day**

*Luke 1:30*

"And the angel said unto her, Fear not, Mary: for thou has found favour with God."

**Quote of the Day**

*Jeffrey R. Holland, "The Ministry of Angels," October 2008*

"Usually [angels] are *not* seen. Sometimes they are. But seen or unseen they are *always* near. Sometimes their assignments are very grand and have significance for the whole world. Sometimes their messages are more private. Occasionally the angelic purpose is to warn. But most often it is to comfort, to provide some form of merciful attention, guidance in difficult times."

HOW DID GOD SHOW UP FOR YOU TODAY?

WHAT CAN YOU ASK CHRIST TO HELP YOU CARRY RIGHT NOW?

WHAT IS YOUR HOPE FOR TOMORROW?

DATE    /    /

## Scripture of the Day

*2 Nephi 32:9*

"I say unto you that ye must pray always, and not faint; that ye must not perform any thing unto the Lord save in the first place ye shall pray unto the Father in the name of Christ, that he will consecrate thy performance unto thee, that thy performance may be for the welfare of thy soul."

## Quote of the Day

*Henry B. Eyring, "The Faith to Ask and Then to Act," October 2021*

"If your faith in Jesus Christ has led to a heart softened through the effects of His Atonement, you will be more able to feel the whisperings of the Spirit in answer to your prayers. My personal experience is that the still, small voice—which is real—is clear and discernible in my mind when I feel an internal quiet and submission to the Lord's will."

### HOW DID GOD SHOW UP FOR YOU TODAY?

### WHAT CAN YOU ASK CHRIST TO HELP YOU CARRY RIGHT NOW?

### WHAT IS YOUR HOPE FOR TOMORROW?

DATE    /    /

## Scripture of the Day
*Alma 1:30*

"And thus, in their prosperous circumstances, they did not send away any who were naked, or that were hungry, or that were athirst, or that were sick, or that had not been nourished; and they did not set their hearts upon riches; therefore they were liberal to all, both old and young, both bond and free, both male and female, whether out of the church or in the church, having no respect to persons as to those who stood in need."

## Quote of the Day
*Sharon Eubank, "I Pray He'll Use Us," October 2021*

"Brothers and sisters, through your ministry, donations, time, and love, you have been the answer to so many prayers. And yet there is so much more to do. As baptized members of the Church, we are under covenant to care for those in need. Our individual efforts don't necessarily require money or faraway locations; they do require the guidance of the Holy Spirit and a willing heart."

### HOW DID GOD SHOW UP FOR YOU TODAY?

### WHAT CAN YOU ASK CHRIST TO HELP YOU CARRY RIGHT NOW?

### WHAT IS YOUR HOPE FOR TOMORROW?

DATE      /      /

## Scripture of the Day

*Matthew 14:28–31*

"And Peter answered him and said, Lord, if it be thou, bid me come unto thee on the water. And he said, Come. And when Peter was come down out of the ship, he walked on the water, to go to Jesus. But when he saw the wind boisterous, he was afraid; and beginning to sink, he cried, saying, Lord, save me. And immediately Jesus stretched forth his hand, and caught him, and said unto him, O thou of little faith, wherefore didst thou doubt?"

## Quote of the Day

*Jonathan S. Schmitt, "That They Might Know Thee," October 2022*

"When our faith falters, we can cry out to Jesus, 'Lord, save me,' just like Peter as he began to sink in Galilee's stormy sea. On that day, Jesus reached down to rescue the drowning disciple. He has done the same for me, and He will do the same for you. Don't ever give up on Jesus—He will never give up on you!"

### HOW DID GOD SHOW UP FOR YOU TODAY?

### WHAT CAN YOU ASK CHRIST TO HELP YOU CARRY RIGHT NOW?

### WHAT IS YOUR HOPE FOR TOMORROW?

DATE      /      /

## Scripture of the Day

"The Lord also shall roar out of Zion, and utter his voice from Jerusalem; and the heavens and the earth shall shake: but the Lord will be the hope of his people, and the strength of the children of Israel."

*Joel 3:16*

## Quote of the Day

"Just as Jesus invited each one of the Nephite disciples to feel His wounds, He died for each one of us, personally, as if you or I were the only person on earth. He extends to us a personal invitation to come unto Him and draw upon the marvelous blessings of His Atonement."

*Gérald Caussé, "A Living Witness of the Living Christ," April 2020*

### HOW DID GOD SHOW UP FOR YOU TODAY?

### WHAT CAN YOU ASK CHRIST TO HELP YOU CARRY RIGHT NOW?

### WHAT IS YOUR HOPE FOR TOMORROW?

DATE    /    /

**Scripture of the Day**

3 Nephi 17:6

"And he said unto them: Behold, my bowels are filled with compassion towards you."

**Quote of the Day**

Peter F. Meurs, "He Could Heal Me!" April 2023

"I believe that His compassion was much more than a response to the people's tears. It seems that He could see them through the eyes of His atoning sacrifice. He saw their every pain, affliction, and temptation. He saw their sicknesses. He saw their infirmities, and He knew from His agonizing suffering in Gethsemane and on Golgotha how to succor them according to their infirmities. Similarly, when our Savior, Jesus Christ, looks upon us, He sees and understands the pain and burden of our sins. He sees our addictions and challenges. He sees our struggles and afflictions of any kind—and He is filled with compassion toward us."

### HOW DID GOD SHOW UP FOR YOU TODAY?

### WHAT CAN YOU ASK CHRIST TO HELP YOU CARRY RIGHT NOW?

### WHAT IS YOUR HOPE FOR TOMORROW?

DATE        /        /

## Scripture of the Day

"Forasmuch as ye are manifestly declared to be the epistle of Christ ministered by us, written not with ink, but with the Spirit of the living God; not in tables of stone, but in fleshy tables of the heart."

*2 Corinthians 3:3*

## Quote of the Day

"As disciples of Jesus Christ, we are to be examples of how to interact with others—especially when we have differences of opinion. One of the easiest ways to identify a *true follower* of Jesus Christ is how compassionately that person treats other people."

*Russell M. Nelson, "Peacemakers Needed," April 2023*

### HOW DID GOD SHOW UP FOR YOU TODAY?

### WHAT CAN YOU ASK CHRIST TO HELP YOU CARRY RIGHT NOW?

### WHAT IS YOUR HOPE FOR TOMORROW?

DATE  /  /

### Scripture of the Day

*2 Nephi 2:25*

"Adam fell that men might be; and men are, that they might have joy."

### Quote of the Day

*Joseph W. Sitati, "Patterns of Discipleship," October 2022*

"Whenever we care to notice, we see that Heavenly Father has given us sufficient witnesses of truth to govern our lives so we will know Him and have the blessings of peace and joy."

#### HOW DID GOD SHOW UP FOR YOU TODAY?

#### WHAT CAN YOU ASK CHRIST TO HELP YOU CARRY RIGHT NOW?

#### WHAT IS YOUR HOPE FOR TOMORROW?

DATE    /    /

## Scripture of the Day

*3 Nephi 9:15*

"Behold, I am Jesus Christ the Son of God. I created the heavens and the earth, and all things that in them are. I was with the Father from the beginning. I am in the Father, and the Father in me; and in me hath the Father glorified his name."

## Quote of the Day

*Milton Camargo, "Focus on Jesus Christ," April 2023*

"The Lord Jesus Christ lives today. He can be an active, daily presence in our lives. He is the solution to our problems, but we must lift our eyes and raise our sights to see Him."

### HOW DID GOD SHOW UP FOR YOU TODAY?

### WHAT CAN YOU ASK CHRIST TO HELP YOU CARRY RIGHT NOW?

### WHAT IS YOUR HOPE FOR TOMORROW?

DATE      /      /

## Scripture of the Day

"Till we all come in the unity of the faith, and of the knowledge of the Son of God, unto a perfect man, unto the measure of the stature of the fulness of Christ."

*Ephesians 4:13*

## Quote of the Day

"The point is that faith means trusting God in good times and bad, even if that includes some suffering until we see His arm revealed in our behalf. That can be difficult in our modern world when many have come to believe that the highest good in life is to avoid all suffering, that no one should ever anguish over anything. But that belief will never lead us to 'the measure of the stature of the fulness of Christ.'"

*Jeffrey R. Holland, "Waiting on the Lord," October 2020*

### HOW DID GOD SHOW UP FOR YOU TODAY?

### WHAT CAN YOU ASK CHRIST TO HELP YOU CARRY RIGHT NOW?

### WHAT IS YOUR HOPE FOR TOMORROW?

DATE      /      /

## Scripture of the Day

"And we talk of Christ, we rejoice in Christ, we preach of Christ, we prophesy of Christ, and we write according to our prophecies, that our children may know to what source they may look for a remission of their sins."

*2 Nephi 25:26*

## Quote of the Day

"The Church is a gathering place for imperfect individuals who love God and who are willing to follow the Lord Jesus Christ. That willingness is rooted in the reality that Jesus is the Christ, the Son of the living God."

*Kevin W. Pearson, "Are You Still Willing?" October 2022*

### HOW DID GOD SHOW UP FOR YOU TODAY?

### WHAT CAN YOU ASK CHRIST TO HELP YOU CARRY RIGHT NOW?

### WHAT IS YOUR HOPE FOR TOMORROW?

DATE     /     /

## *Scripture of the Day*

*Jacob 2:17*

"Think of your brethren like unto yourselves, and be familiar with all and free with your substance, that they may be rich like unto you."

## *Quote of the Day*

*Sharon Eubank, "By Union of Feeling We Obtain Power with God," October 2020*

This world isn't what I want it to be. There are many things I want to influence and make better. And frankly, there is a lot of opposition to what I hope for, and sometimes I feel powerless. Lately, I have been asking myself searching questions: How can I understand people around me better? How will I create that 'union of feeling' when all are so different? What power from God might I access if I am just a little bit more unified with others?

#### HOW DID GOD SHOW UP FOR YOU TODAY?

#### WHAT CAN YOU ASK CHRIST TO HELP YOU CARRY RIGHT NOW?

#### WHAT IS YOUR HOPE FOR TOMORROW?

DATE      /      /

**Scripture of the Day**

"And I will pray the Father, and he shall give you another Comforter, that he may abide with you for ever; . . . I will not leave you comfortless: I will come to you."

*John 14:16, 18*

**Quote of the Day**

"My brothers and sisters, I plead with you to make time for the Lord! Make your own spiritual foundation firm and able to stand the test of time by doing those things that allow the Holy Ghost to be with you always."

*Russell M. Nelson, "Make Time for the Lord," October 2021*

### HOW DID GOD SHOW UP FOR YOU TODAY?

### WHAT CAN YOU ASK CHRIST TO HELP YOU CARRY RIGHT NOW?

### WHAT IS YOUR HOPE FOR TOMORROW?

DATE      /      /

## Scripture of the Day

*Mosiah 5:15*

"Be steadfast and immovable, always abounding in good works, that Christ, the Lord God Omnipotent, may seal you his, that you may be brought to heaven, that ye may have everlasting salvation and eternal life, through the wisdom, and power, and justice, and mercy of him who created all things, in heaven and in earth, who is God above all."

## Quote of the Day

*Neil L. Andersen, "My Mind Caught Hold upon This Thought of Jesus Christ," April 2023*

"By focusing our attention on Jesus Christ, all else around us—while still present—is viewed through our love for Him. Less important distractions fade, and we remove those things that are not in keeping with His light and character."

### HOW DID GOD SHOW UP FOR YOU TODAY?

### WHAT CAN YOU ASK CHRIST TO HELP YOU CARRY RIGHT NOW?

### WHAT IS YOUR HOPE FOR TOMORROW?

DATE       /       /

**Scripture of the Day**

*1 Nephi 3:7*

"And it came to pass that I, Nephi, said unto my father: I will go and do the things which the Lord hath commanded, for I know that the Lord giveth no commandments unto the children of men, save he shall prepare a way for them that they may accomplish the thing which he commandeth them."

**Quote of the Day**

*Larry S. Kacher,
"Ladder of Faith,"
April 2022*

"As our faith in the Savior increases, we observe a subtle shift that includes a divine understanding of our relationship with God—a steady movement away from 'What do I want?' to 'What does God want?' Like the Savior, we want to act 'not as I will, but as thou wilt.' We want to do God's work and be an instrument in His hands."

### HOW DID GOD SHOW UP FOR YOU TODAY?

### WHAT CAN YOU ASK CHRIST TO HELP YOU CARRY RIGHT NOW?

### WHAT IS YOUR HOPE FOR TOMORROW?

DATE      /      /

## Scripture of the Day

*1 Corinthians 11:28*

"But let a man examine himself, and so let him eat of that bread, and drink of that cup."

## Quote of the Day

*Milton Camargo, "Focus on Jesus Christ," April 2023*

"Renewing our covenants during the sacrament each Sunday is a great opportunity to examine ourselves and refocus our lives on Jesus Christ. By partaking of the sacrament, we declare that we do 'always remember him.' The word *always* is so significant. It extends the Savior's influence into every part of our lives. We don't remember Him only at church or only during our morning prayers or only when we're in trouble and we need something. Yes, we sometimes get distracted. We forget. We lose our focus. But renewing our covenants means that we want to always remember the Savior, that we will try to do so throughout the week, and that we will recommit and refocus on Him again at the sacrament table next week."

### HOW DID GOD SHOW UP FOR YOU TODAY?

### WHAT CAN YOU ASK CHRIST TO HELP YOU CARRY RIGHT NOW?

### WHAT IS YOUR HOPE FOR TOMORROW?

DATE    /    /

## Scripture of the Day

*Mosiah 15:8–9*

"And thus God breaketh the bands of death, having gained the victory over death; giving the Son power to make intercession for the children of men—having ascended into heaven, having the bowels of mercy; being filled with compassion towards the children of men; standing betwixt them and justice; having broken the bands of death, taken upon himself their iniquity and their transgressions, having redeemed them, and satisfied the demands of justice."

## Quote of the Day

*Peter F. Meurs, "He Could Heal Me!" April 2023*

"Whether you are carrying the burden of unresolved sin, suffering because of an offense committed against you long ago, or struggling to forgive yourself for an accidental mistake, you have access to the healing and redeeming power of the Savior Jesus Christ."

### HOW DID GOD SHOW UP FOR YOU TODAY?

### WHAT CAN YOU ASK CHRIST TO HELP YOU CARRY RIGHT NOW?

### WHAT IS YOUR HOPE FOR TOMORROW?

DATE    /    /

### Scripture of the Day

*2 Nephi 2:8*

"Wherefore, how great the importance to make these things known unto the inhabitants of the earth, that they may know that there is no flesh that can dwell in the presence of God, save it be through the merits, and mercy, and grace of the Holy Messiah, who layeth down his life according to the flesh, and taketh it again by the power of the Spirit, that he may bring to pass the resurrection of the dead, being the first that should rise."

### Quote of the Day

*Marcus B. Nash, "Hold Up Your Light," October 2021*

"In Christ these good tidings are preached to the meek; in Christ are the brokenhearted bound up; in Christ is liberty proclaimed to the captives; and in Christ, only in Christ, are those who mourn given beauty for ashes. Hence, the great need to make these things known!"

#### HOW DID GOD SHOW UP FOR YOU TODAY?

#### WHAT CAN YOU ASK CHRIST TO HELP YOU CARRY RIGHT NOW?

#### WHAT IS YOUR HOPE FOR TOMORROW?

DATE    /    /

## Scripture of the Day

"Peace I leave with you, my peace I give unto you: not as the world giveth, give I unto you. Let not your heart be troubled, neither let it be afraid."

*John 14:27*

## Quote of the Day

"As my love for the Savior has grown, so has my desire to replace hurt and anger with His healing balm. It has been a process of many years, requiring courage, vulnerability, perseverance, and learning to trust in the Savior's divine power to save and heal."

*Kristin M. Yee, "Beauty for Ashes: The Healing Path of Forgiveness," October 2022*

### HOW DID GOD SHOW UP FOR YOU TODAY?

### WHAT CAN YOU ASK CHRIST TO HELP YOU CARRY RIGHT NOW?

### WHAT IS YOUR HOPE FOR TOMORROW?

DATE    /    /

## *Scripture of the Day*

*Matthew 17:20*

"If ye have faith as a grain of mustard seed, ye shall say unto this mountain, Remove hence to yonder place; and it shall remove; and nothing shall be impossible unto you."

## *Quote of the Day*

*Russell M. Nelson, "Christ Is Risen; Faith in Him Will Move Mountains," April 2021*

"*Start today* to increase your faith. Through your faith, Jesus Christ will increase your ability to move the mountains in your life, even though your personal challenges may loom as large as Mount Everest."

### HOW DID GOD SHOW UP FOR YOU TODAY?

### WHAT CAN YOU ASK CHRIST TO HELP YOU CARRY RIGHT NOW?

### WHAT IS YOUR HOPE FOR TOMORROW?

DATE    /    /

## Scripture of the Day

"The good shepherd doth call you; yea, and in his own name he doth call you, which is the name of Christ."

*Alma 5:38*

## Quote of the Day

"The Lord wants us to become holy, to be possessed of charity, and to come to know Him. . . . Ultimately, the Lord wants our hearts; He wants us to become new creatures in Christ."

*L. Todd Budge, "Giving Holiness to the Lord," October 2021*

### HOW DID GOD SHOW UP FOR YOU TODAY?

### WHAT CAN YOU ASK CHRIST TO HELP YOU CARRY RIGHT NOW?

### WHAT IS YOUR HOPE FOR TOMORROW?

DATE     /     /

## *Scripture of the Day*

*Mark 9:7*

"And there was a cloud that overshadowed them: and a voice came out of the cloud, saying, This is my beloved Son: hear him."

## *Quote of the Day*

*Neil L. Andersen, "We Talk of Christ," October 2020*

"Like a guiding star in a clear, dark sky, Jesus Christ lights our way. He came to earth in a humble stable. He lived a perfect life. He healed the sick and raised the dead. He was a friend to the forgotten. He taught us to do good, to obey, and to love one another. He was crucified on a cross, rising majestically three days later, allowing us and those we love to live beyond the grave. With His incomparable mercy and grace, He took upon Himself our sins and our suffering, bringing forgiveness as we repent and peace in the storms of life. We love Him. We worship Him. We follow Him. He is the anchor of our souls."

### HOW DID GOD SHOW UP FOR YOU TODAY?

### WHAT CAN YOU ASK CHRIST TO HELP YOU CARRY RIGHT NOW?

### WHAT IS YOUR HOPE FOR TOMORROW?

DATE    /    /

## Scripture of the Day

*1 Peter 3:15*

"But sanctify the Lord God in your hearts: and be ready always to give an answer to every man that asketh you a reason of the hope that is in you with meekness and fear."

## Quote of the Day

*M. Russell Ballard, "Hope in Christ," April 2021*

"I speak of hope in Christ not as wishful thinking. Instead, I speak of hope as an expectation that will be realized. Such hope is essential to overcoming adversity, fostering spiritual resilience and strength, and coming to know that we are loved by our Eternal Father and that we are His children, who belong to His family."

### HOW DID GOD SHOW UP FOR YOU TODAY?

### WHAT CAN YOU ASK CHRIST TO HELP YOU CARRY RIGHT NOW?

### WHAT IS YOUR HOPE FOR TOMORROW?

DATE ____ / ____ / ____

## Scripture of the Day

*3 Nephi 27:13–14*

"Behold I have given unto you my gospel, and this is the gospel which I have given unto you—that I came into the world to do the will of my Father, because my Father sent me. And my Father sent me that I might be lifted up upon the cross; and after that I had been lifted up upon the cross, that I might draw all men unto me, that as I have been lifted up by men even so should men be lifted up by the Father, to stand before me, to be judged of their works, whether they be good or whether they be evil."

## Quote of the Day

*Mark A. Bragg, "Christlike Poise," April 2023*

"The enabling power of Christ, made possible by His atoning sacrifice, gives us the strength to endure and prevail. Because of Jesus Christ we can covenant with God and be strengthened in keeping that covenant. We can be bound to the Savior in joy and calm, regardless of our temporal circumstances."

### HOW DID GOD SHOW UP FOR YOU TODAY?

### WHAT CAN YOU ASK CHRIST TO HELP YOU CARRY RIGHT NOW?

### WHAT IS YOUR HOPE FOR TOMORROW?

DATE       /       /

## Scripture of the Day

*Matthew 25:35–40*

"For I was an hungred, and ye gave me meat: I was thirsty, and ye gave me drink: I was a stranger, and ye took me in: Naked, and ye clothed me: I was sick, and ye visited me: I was in prison, and ye came unto me. Then shall the righteous answer him, saying, Lord, when saw we thee an hungred, and fed thee? or thirsty, and gave thee drink? When saw we thee a stranger, and took thee in? or naked, and clothed thee? Or when saw we thee sick, or in prison, and came unto thee? And the King shall answer and say unto them, Verily I say unto you, Inasmuch as ye have done it unto one of the least of these my brethren, ye have done it unto me."

## Quote of the Day

*L. Todd Budge, "Giving Holiness to the Lord," October 2021*

"When our sacrifices on behalf of others are viewed from the perspective of 'giving up,' we may see them as a burden and become discouraged when our sacrifices are not recognized or rewarded. However, when viewed from the perspective of 'giving to' the Lord, our sacrifices on behalf of others become gifts, and the joy of generously giving becomes its own reward."

### HOW DID GOD SHOW UP FOR YOU TODAY?

### WHAT CAN YOU ASK CHRIST TO HELP YOU CARRY RIGHT NOW?

### WHAT IS YOUR HOPE FOR TOMORROW?

DATE      /      /

## Scripture of the Day

*Luke 6:45*

"A good man out of the good treasure of his heart bringeth forth that which is good; and an evil man out of the evil treasure of his heart bringeth forth that which is evil: for of the abundance of the heart his mouth speaketh."

## Quote of the Day

*Neil L. Andersen, "My Mind Caught Hold upon This Thought of Jesus Christ," April 2023*

"In this mortal life, our mind and spirit need exceptional attention. Our mind allows us to live, to choose, and to discern good and evil. Our spirit receives the confirming witness that God is our Father, that Jesus Christ is the Son of God, and that Their teachings are our guide to happiness here and eternal life beyond the grave."

### HOW DID GOD SHOW UP FOR YOU TODAY?

### WHAT CAN YOU ASK CHRIST TO HELP YOU CARRY RIGHT NOW?

### WHAT IS YOUR HOPE FOR TOMORROW?

DATE      /      /

## *Scripture of the Day*

*Alma 5:45–46*

"And this is not all. Do ye not suppose that I know of these things myself? Behold, I testify unto you that I do know that these things whereof I have spoken are true. And how do ye suppose that I know of their surety? Behold, I say unto you they are made known unto me by the Holy Spirit of God. Behold, I have fasted and prayed many days that I might know these things of myself. And now I do know of myself that they are true; for the Lord God hath made them manifest unto me by his Holy Spirit; and this is the spirit of revelation which is in me."

## *Quote of the Day*

*M. Russell Ballard, "Remember What Matters Most," April 2023*

"Faith in Jesus Christ is the foundation of our testimonies. A testimony is a witness or confirmation of eternal truth impressed upon individual hearts and souls through the Holy Ghost. A testimony of Jesus Christ, born of and strengthened by the Spirit, changes lives—it changes the way we think and how we live. A testimony turns us toward our Heavenly Father and His divine Son."

### HOW DID GOD SHOW UP FOR YOU TODAY?

### WHAT CAN YOU ASK CHRIST TO HELP YOU CARRY RIGHT NOW?

### WHAT IS YOUR HOPE FOR TOMORROW?

DATE ____/____/____

## Scripture of the Day

*Revelation 21:4*

"And God shall wipe away all tears from their eyes; and there shall be no more death, neither sorrow, nor crying, neither shall there be any more pain: for the former things are passed away."

## Quote of the Day

*Milton Camargo, "Focus on Jesus Christ," April 2023*

"[These problems include] the tribulations, difficult experiences, sadness, pain, and unfairness of this world. Jesus Christ overcame all of this. For those who strive to follow Him, He will one day 'wipe away all tears' and make things right again. In the meantime, He can strengthen us to pass through our trials with confidence, good cheer, and peace."

### HOW DID GOD SHOW UP FOR YOU TODAY?

### WHAT CAN YOU ASK CHRIST TO HELP YOU CARRY RIGHT NOW?

### WHAT IS YOUR HOPE FOR TOMORROW?

DATE       /       /

## *Scripture of the Day*

*John 21:15*

"So when they had dined, Jesus saith to Simon Peter, Simon, son of Jonas, lovest thou me more than these? He saith unto him, Yea, Lord; thou knowest that I love thee. He saith unto him, Feed my lambs."

## *Quote of the Day*

*M. Russell Ballard, "Lovest Thou Me More Than These?" October 2021*

"How would we answer the question 'Lovest thou me more than these?' When we discover a fuller meaning of this question, we can become better family members, neighbors, citizens, members of the Church, and sons and daughters of God."

### HOW DID GOD SHOW UP FOR YOU TODAY?

### WHAT CAN YOU ASK CHRIST TO HELP YOU CARRY RIGHT NOW?

### WHAT IS YOUR HOPE FOR TOMORROW?

DATE       /       /

## Scripture of the Day

*Alma 36:18–19*

"Now, as my mind caught hold upon this thought, I cried within my heart: O Jesus, thou Son of God, have mercy on me, who am in the gall of bitterness, and am encircled about by the everlasting chains of death. And now, behold, when I thought this, I could remember my pains no more; yea, I was harrowed up by the memory of my sins no more."

## Quote of the Day

*Neil L. Andersen, "My Mind Caught Hold upon This Thought of Jesus Christ," April 2023*

"Alma 'caught hold upon' the truth of Jesus Christ. If we were using the words 'caught hold upon' in a physical sense, we might say, 'He caught hold upon the guardrail just as he was falling,' meaning he reached out suddenly and tightly seized something solidly cemented to a secure foundation. In Alma's case, it was his mind that reached out and secured this powerful truth of Jesus Christ's atoning sacrifice. Acting in faith on that truth, and by the power and grace of God, he was rescued from despair and filled with hope. While our experiences may not be as dramatic as Alma's, they are nonetheless as eternally significant."

### HOW DID GOD SHOW UP FOR YOU TODAY?

### WHAT CAN YOU ASK CHRIST TO HELP YOU CARRY RIGHT NOW?

### WHAT IS YOUR HOPE FOR TOMORROW?

DATE      /      /

## *Scripture of the Day*

"If any of you lack wisdom, let him ask of God, that giveth to all men liberally, and upbraideth not; and it shall be given him."

*James 1:5*

## *Quote of the Day*

"Waiting upon the Lord implies action. I have learned over the years that our hope in Christ increases when we serve others. Serving as Jesus served, we naturally increase our hope in Him. . . . The Lord honors those who serve and wait upon Him in patience and faith."

*M. Russell Ballard,*
*"Hope in Christ,"*
*April 2021*

### HOW DID GOD SHOW UP FOR YOU TODAY?

### WHAT CAN YOU ASK CHRIST TO HELP YOU CARRY RIGHT NOW?

### WHAT IS YOUR HOPE FOR TOMORROW?

DATE    /    /

### Scripture of the Day

*Luke 2:10–11*

"And the angel said unto them, Fear not: for, behold, I bring you good tidings of great joy, which shall be to all people. For unto you is born this day in the city of David a Saviour, which is Christ the Lord."

### Quote of the Day

*Michael John U. Teh, "Our Personal Savior," April 2021*

"An increasing understanding that the Atonement of Jesus Christ applies to us personally and individually will help us know Him. Oftentimes it is easier for us to think and speak of Christ's Atonement in general terms than to recognize its personal significance in our lives. The Atonement of Jesus Christ is infinite and eternal and all-encompassing in its breadth and depth but wholly personal and individual in its effects. Because of His atoning sacrifice, the Savior has power to cleanse, heal, and strengthen us one by one."

**HOW DID GOD SHOW UP FOR YOU TODAY?**

**WHAT CAN YOU ASK CHRIST TO HELP YOU CARRY RIGHT NOW?**

**WHAT IS YOUR HOPE FOR TOMORROW?**

DATE      /      /

## *Scripture of the Day*

"Behold, my soul delighteth in the things of the Lord; and my heart pondereth continually upon the things which I have seen and heard."

*2 Nephi 4:16*

## *Quote of the Day*

"To be most effective, your experiences with the scriptures must be your own. Reading or hearing about another person's experiences and insights can be helpful, but that won't bring the same converting power. There is no substitute for the time *you* spend in the scriptures, hearing the Holy Ghost speak directly to *you*."

*Mark L. Pace, "Conversion Is Our Goal," April 2022*

### HOW DID GOD SHOW UP FOR YOU TODAY?

### WHAT CAN YOU ASK CHRIST TO HELP YOU CARRY RIGHT NOW?

### WHAT IS YOUR HOPE FOR TOMORROW?

DATE     /     /

### *Scripture of the Day*

*Luke 22:44*

"And being in an agony he prayed more earnestly: and his sweat was as it were great drops of blood falling down to the ground."

### *Quote of the Day*

*Mark A. Bragg,
"Christlike Poise,"
April 2023*

"Under the immense pressure to enable the salvation of all humankind, Jesus demonstrated three important conditions that help us understand His great poise. First, He knew who He was and was true to His divine mission. Next, He knew that there was a great plan of happiness. And finally, He knew that through His infinite Atonement, all who faithfully yoke themselves to Him by making and keeping sacred covenants received through priesthood ordinances will be saved."

#### HOW DID GOD SHOW UP FOR YOU TODAY?

#### WHAT CAN YOU ASK CHRIST TO HELP YOU CARRY RIGHT NOW?

#### WHAT IS YOUR HOPE FOR TOMORROW?

DATE         /         /

**Scripture of the Day**

*Luke 21:36*

"Watch ye therefore, and pray always, that ye may be accounted worthy to escape all these things that shall come to pass, and to stand before the Son of man."

**Quote of the Day**

*M. Russell Ballard, "Watch Ye Therefore, and Pray Always," October 2020*

"The Savior taught us to not limit who we pray for. . . . Sincerely praying for those who may be considered our enemies demonstrates our belief that God can change our hearts and the hearts of others. Such prayers should strengthen our resolve to make whatever changes are necessary in our own lives, families, and communities."

### HOW DID GOD SHOW UP FOR YOU TODAY?

### WHAT CAN YOU ASK CHRIST TO HELP YOU CARRY RIGHT NOW?

### WHAT IS YOUR HOPE FOR TOMORROW?

DATE    /    /

## Scripture of the Day

*Mosiah 27:25–26*

"And the Lord said unto me: Marvel not that all mankind, yea, men and women, all nations, kindreds, tongues and people, must be born again; yea, born of God, changed from their carnal and fallen state, to a state of righteousness, being redeemed of God, becoming his sons and daughters; and thus they become new creatures; and unless they do this, they can in nowise inherit the kingdom of God."

## Quote of the Day

*Milton Camargo, "Focus on Jesus Christ," April 2023*

"The change that Jesus Christ brings is 'a mighty change.' He changes our very natures; we become 'new creatures.'"

### HOW DID GOD SHOW UP FOR YOU TODAY?

### WHAT CAN YOU ASK CHRIST TO HELP YOU CARRY RIGHT NOW?

### WHAT IS YOUR HOPE FOR TOMORROW?

DATE    /    /

## *Scripture of the Day*

*Mark 4:40*

"And he said unto them, Why are ye so fearful? how is it that ye have no faith?"

## *Quote of the Day*

*Mark A. Bragg, "Christlike Poise," April 2023*

"May we seek the blessings of Christlike poise, not only to help ourselves in challenging times but to bless others and help them through the storms in their lives."

### HOW DID GOD SHOW UP FOR YOU TODAY?

### WHAT CAN YOU ASK CHRIST TO HELP YOU CARRY RIGHT NOW?

### WHAT IS YOUR HOPE FOR TOMORROW?

DATE      /      /

## Scripture of the Day

John 11:39, 43–44

"Jesus said, Take ye away the stone. Martha, the sister of him that was dead, saith unto him, Lord, by this time he stinketh: for he hath been dead four days. . . . And when he thus had spoken, he cried with a loud voice, Lazarus, come forth. And he that was dead came forth, bound hand and foot with graveclothes: and his face was bound about with a napkin. Jesus saith unto them, Loose him, and let him go."

## Quote of the Day

W. Mark Bassett, "After the Fourth Day," April 2023

"Each of these three things had something in common—none required the use of Christ's divine power. That which His disciples could do, He instructed *them* to do. . . . However, it was only the Christ who had the power and authority to raise Lazarus from the dead. My impression is that the Savior expects us to do all we can do, and He will do what *only He* can do."

### HOW DID GOD SHOW UP FOR YOU TODAY?

### WHAT CAN YOU ASK CHRIST TO HELP YOU CARRY RIGHT NOW?

### WHAT IS YOUR HOPE FOR TOMORROW?